FODEN EXPORT VEHICLES

This book is dedicated to friend and countryman René Megens, who sadly passed away in 2011 at the age of only 50. Rene was the archivist of the Haukes transport company. He provided me with very useful information on Dutch Fodens and with many interesting photographs.

Cover: A good-looking 6AXB6/40 model double drive tractor unit fitted with a fibreglass S21 cab featuring a sleeper extension and double roof. It was powered by a Gardner 6LXB-180 engine and pulls a Freighter semi-trailer fitted with a Transicold Freezer installation. Gascoyne Trading used this combination for transporting fresh produce in Western Australia in the 1960s. *(Niels Jansen collection)*

FODEN EXPORT VEHICLES

Wobbe Reitsma

Old Pond
PUBLISHING

First published 2017

Copyright © Wobbe Reitsma 2017

Published by
Old Pond Publishing,
An imprint of 5M Publishing Ltd,
Benchmark House,
8 Smithy Wood Drive,
Sheffield, S35 1QN, UK
Tel: +44 (0) 0114 246 4799
www.oldpond.com

A catalogue record for this book is available from the British Library

ISBN 9781910456767

Book layout by Servis Filmsetting Ltd, Stockport, Cheshire
Printed by Replika Printing Ltd, Pvt India

Contents

Introduction

Foden already sold steamers in substantial numbers to Australia, South Africa and Argentina before World War II. However, Foden's export business became really important after this war, when many countries needed new vehicles in order to replace destroyed and worn out lorries. Great Britain was happy to oblige because most British lorry factories were still producing. Diesel engines were the name of the game now and Gardner engines soon became available again in decent numbers. In the first years after this war there were enough redundant British and US army vehicles to fulfil the needs of lots of transport companies all over the world. But these vehicles were not designed to take heavy loads and most were still powered by petrol engines. The British lorry manufacturers had been

working on new designs during and directly after the war. Most were able to offer new civilian designs from 1948 onwards.

Just after the war the British government had introduced a rationing system for many raw materials that were necessary to build lorries. Manufacturers were supposed to export at least half of their production in order to be allocated the wanted raw materials. As a result, exporting vehicles became an incentive to build enough vehicles for the British home market. Most export Fodens went to countries that were part of the British Empire or countries that became independent from Great Britain in the 1950s and 1960s. Strong export markets were retained in countries that were part of the British Commonwealth.

Exports were special vehicles, which differed greatly from the designs used in Great Britain. In many countries around the world, gross weights of vehicles exceeded the British values significantly. So, the majority of Foden export vehicles had much stronger chassis, gearboxes, axles, suspensions and more powerful engines. To keep the heat out of the cabs they needed tropical double roofs. Sleeper cabs also became an option in many export markets from the 1950s onwards.

Foden chassis featuring the new S18 cab, which was introduced in 1948, were quite promising export models. They soon became very popular in European countries including Holland, Belgium and Portugal, but also in South Africa, Rhodesia, New Zealand and Australia. Gardner 6LWs powered most exports, but within two years the legendary straight-eight Gardner

Left: Foden advertised its export products in many commercial vehicle publications, such as *Commercial Motor.* This weekly transport magazine issued a special export edition in April 1951, in which Foden advertised its new FGD6 dump truck and FG8/15 chassis fitted with the new eight-cylinder Gardner 8LW. This powerful eight-in-line diesel engine produced 150bhp. The FG8/15 was specially designed for export markets. Many of them were exported to Australia and South Africa, but also to European countries. *(Author's collection)*

8LW, producing 150bhp, became available. As a result, many exports were fitted with this powerful engine. Foden established and appointed importers in many parts of the world in the 1950s to sell its products and provide the necessary service and support to customers. Foden appointed agents in nearly every West European country during the 1950s. To save transport costs as well as import duties, Foden even set up a full vehicle assembly plant in South Africa in 1950. Export vehicles, including heavy 6×4 tractor units and special 8×4 rigid chassis, were exhibited during important commercial vehicle shows in Great Britain at Earls Court in London in 1954, 1956 and 1958. Foden also started to export specialist vehicles such as dump trucks, aircraft refuellers, crane carriers and even coach and bus chassis.

The demand for Foden trucks in Europe declined in the 1960s. The reason was the rise of the European truck building industry. Foden had to compete with European truck factories including DAF, Scania–Vabis, Volvo, Mercedes–Benz, Fiat and many others. These companies offered good quality products that were equal and, in many cases, more suitable for the European market than British products. Exports of dump trucks and crane carriers into Europe made a remarkable exception to the general rule that Foden products were less wanted. Nevertheless, Foden kept strong footholds in Africa, Australia and New Zealand. Export markets in the Middle East and Asia also started to be good sources of business, thanks to the oil industry boom in that part of the world during the 1970s. Gardner was no longer the sole provider of heavy engines in Foden chassis. At the end of the 1950s the powerful Rolls–Royce engine became a much appreciated power plant. In some countries, such as New Zealand, Foden's own two-stroke engines were also quite popular, and Cummins engines became even more successful from the early 1960s onwards. A special steel cab for export purposes was introduced in 1968. These steel S40 and S41 cabs, manufactured by Motor Panels, were fitted to many export vehicles well into the 1970s.

Opposite: Holland was an important export country for Foden trucks during the late 1940s and 1950s. The majority were sold to brick hauliers, who appreciated the strong chassis and reliable Gardner engines. The standard S18 cabs were less appreciated as they were draughty and cold in wintertime, while being very hot in summers. Two brick carriers leave a Dutch brick works fully loaded with clinkers during the late 1950s. The vehicle on the left is a 1956 model FG6/12 fitted with a Dutch coach-built cab manufactured by Paul & van Weelde. The other vehicle, a 1957 FG6/20 model, is fitted with a British-built Boalloy cab. Both vehicles had Gardner 6LW engines, producing 112bhp. *(Author's collection)*

Left: South Africa was another major export market for Foden, which had its own local assembly plant during the 1970s and early 1980s. This is an early 1970s model 4AC6/35 tractor unit, powered by a Cummins engine and fitted with a locally built sleeper cab, which featured some S40 cab parts and front mudguards. *(Author's collection)*

In the early 1970s Foden tried to regain part of the European truck market by introducing a new and very promising truck series called the Universal. It was introduced and exhibited during the 1974 Amsterdam RAI Show. These vehicles were fitted with steel Motor Panels S90 cabs, which also became available in sleeper cab form. Unfortunately the Universal series did not turn out to be the success that Foden had expected, however, towards the end of the 1970s these export series, which were now called Super Haulmasters, became very successful in the Middle East. In 1977 a little more than 25 per cent of Foden's production was sold to countries in Africa and the Middle East. Exports to Europe, Asia and Australia had dwindled to a mere 2 per cent.

After Foden went bankrupt in 1980 it was bought out by American company Paccar. The new company decided that Foden should concentrate on the British market. As a result, most Foden specialist vehicles, such as dump trucks and buses, were removed from Foden's catalogues. Foden's export markets diminished and sales were mainly concentrated on South Africa, Israel and New Zealand. S106T double drive tractor units and S108 8×4 rigids were the best-selling models in these markets. Exports to Australia and the Middle East had virtually ceased completely.

With the introduction of the 4000 series in 1987 Foden made another attempt to conquer a part of the European truck market. In 1988 Paccar Europe, situated in Brussels, announced that Foden was going to put some demonstration vehicles into transport fleets of Dutch and Belgium-based companies. However, it would take until the early 1990s before the Foden 4000 series was actually sold to transport companies in Belgium, France, Spain and Switzerland. The Swiss importer, Friderici, took quite a lot of vehicles, which nearly all went into its own transport fleet. New Zealand was still a major country for Foden exports throughout the 1990s, although total sales of heavy trucks in this part of the world were fewer than 500 units a year. Average export sales to Europe, the Middle East, South Africa and New Zealand were around 100 vehicles a year (about 8–10 per cent of Foden's annual production) during the 1990s, with about half of these going to New Zealand.

Foden finally ceased production of the 4000 series at Sandbach, Cheshire, in 2001. Production of the new Alpha series, which was introduced in 1998, was transferred to Paccar's Leyland plant. The only export market still in existence at the time was New Zealand, where Foden sold the new Alpha in significant numbers. They were quite popular in 8×4 drawbar configuration and in 6×4 tractor–trailer combination. It was not a surprise that Foden sales improved dramatically when competitor ERF pulled out of the New Zealand market in 2001. The new, second generation, Alpha range, fitted with an adapted DAF CF cab, was introduced in New Zealand in May 2003. They were offered until 2006 in 6×4 and 8×4 rigid, but also in 6×4 and 8×4 tractor unit versions, specifically tailored to the operator's needs.

After ceasing production of Foden vehicles at the Leyland plant many second-hand British Foden trucks were exported to countries all over the world. People should not be surprised to see Foden vehicles still working hard in countries in South America, the Caribbean, Africa and even in Eastern Europe.

Acknowledgements

I am fortunate that many people have contributed to this book by providing useful information and suitable photographs. One of my best friends and a dedicated Foden man is John Sanderson, who has allowed me to use his extensive Foden archives to do the necessary research. Long-time truck journalist and photographer Niels Jansen, who I have known for more than thirty years, has also provided me with many interesting Foden photographs for this export volume.

Sincere thanks also go to Yves Ballenegger, Armand Bastin, Richard Blokker, David Bloor, the late Govert Bouthoorn, Arie van den Brand, Rufus Carr, Dennis Child, Pat Crang, Fletcher Challenge Archives, Ian Gallimore, Globetrucker organisation, Julian Hollinshead, Arthur Ingram, Leo Jacobse, Leonard Looijenga, Lex Meeder, the late René Megens, Ian Moxon, Tony Petch, Peter Seaword, Colin Stone, Richard Tew, Peter Tulloch, Ben Uncles and the late Henk Veldkamp for supplying information and photographs.

I have acknowledged the use of the photographs in the captions by naming the photographers as much as possible. I like to stress that I have bought, swapped and collected Foden photographs for more than thirty-five years, but unfortunately many people did not put their names and addresses on the back. In many cases it was not possible to track down where they came from. These photographs have been recorded in this book as coming from the author's collection. If you spot a photograph that is yours, do get in touch with either me or the publisher and we will be happy to credit you properly should the book go into a reprint.

I would also like to thank all the Dutch Foden operators who I spoke to in the 1980s and 1990s. Most of them were willing to tell their stories to me. This and the photographs that were kindly given to me have contributed to a very interesting insight into how Fodens performed in the Dutch haulage scene in the 1950s and early 1960s.

Finally, readers will find comprehensive appendixes for vehicle designation, cab recognition and engines built into Foden vehicles in my previous book *Foden Special Vehicles*, which was published by Roundoak Publishing in 2012 (ISBN 978-1-871565-55-3).

Happy reading!

Wobbe Reitsma
Heerenveen, The Netherlands
September 2016

CHAPTER ONE

Holland

Post-War Activities

Exports Europe

In the first years after World War II, Holland had a shortage of nearly all the basic necessities of life. There was also a great demand for trucks to transport the goods that became available again. Occupying German forces had requisitioned almost all Dutch commercial vehicles. In the last months of the war, when the Germans were anxious to retreat in the direction of their own country, they took any means of transport they could lay their hands on. So, in May 1945 there were not many cars, trucks, buses or even bicycles left in Holland. Fortunately, the liberating forces from Britain, the USA and Canada left lots of army trucks behind when they returned to their own countries.

Thousands of Mack N-series, American and Canadian Fords, Chevrolets, Dodges, GMCs, Bedford O and QL types, FWDs, Diamond Ts and even some Foden DG 6/12s were handed over to the Dutch government.

These trucks were distributed among the Dutch haulage companies, who needed them urgently. Of course, the army trucks had to be adjusted to the requirements of the transport companies. Quite a few were converted into tractor units, others got diesel engines under their bonnets and many were going to pull drawbar trailers. Thanks to those ex-army trucks, the Dutch were transporting goods all over Europe again within a few years after that disastrous war. In 1948 some Dutch haulage companies had enough money to buy new vehicles again.

It was in that year that a Dutchman imported the first ever Foden from Sandbach. The vehicle was shipped from England in a couple of huge wooden crates in c.k.d. (completely knocked down) form. In those days it was cheaper to import trucks in c.k.d. form than as a complete vehicle due to the lower import duties paid.

The first new Foden in Holland was a FG 4×2 tractor unit, which was fitted with the then-new S18 cab. Van der Scheur Transport of Apeldoorn was so pleased with its Foden tractor that it ordered nine more Fodens in the next ten years. Its Fodens were mainly used for transporting heavy machinery and most of them were coupled to low-loaders.

Left: Former British Army vehicles were operated in Holland just after World War II. The vehicle, a DG6/12 built during the war, was refitted with a roomy Dutch coach-built cab, which was manufactured by Bulthuis, based in the north of Holland near Groningen. The vehicle was not provided with a body yet, but Bulthuis was also able to this job. The vehicle is seen just outside Bulthuis premises and has been delivered to the Smit Brothers from Hoogkerk, a few miles from Groningen city. *(Author's collection)*

Opposite: Van der Scheur transport, based in Apeldoorn, operated this flamboyant FGTU6/20 tractor unit and semi-trailer. It was built in 1951 and fitted with a coach-built cab, manufactured by local coachbuilder Wielens. This cab showed some resemblance with the early DAF cabs, which were introduced in 1949. The Gardner 6LW powered tractor unit pulls a two-axle semi-trailer fitted with large single tyres. The semi-trailer is loaded with a German-built Liebherr crane jib. *(John Sanderson collection)*

First Dutch Importer

It was not until 1950 that DIHAM (Deventer Import and Trading Company) of Deventer was appointed as the first professional importer. The company was established by the De Jong Brothers, who operated a transport company. The first Foden sale was a S18 type 4×2 FGTU5/15 tractor unit, which was assembled in January 1951 and destined for De Jong's own transport business. DIHAM had plans to start a Foden assembly plant for Holland. But DIHAM did not make any further sales over the next year and so in 1952 Foden decided to set up its own business in Holland and as a result Fodenway was founded. The company was based in Heelsum, a small village near Arnhem, and Mr Van Gurp, who had also worked for DIHAM, took on the role of managing director.

From 1953 onwards the Foden business flourished, aided by the sharp economic upturn in Holland and other West European countries at that time. Firstly, there was a very big demand for houses, due to the post-war population explosion. The second reason was the replacement of many houses, which were destroyed during the war. Fodens became very popular with companies that were hauling bricks and building materials.

Big Foden Operator

In 1954 the Haukes company, based in a small village near Nijmegen, purchased its first three Foden FG8/15s. The rigid four-axle vehicles with drop side bodies were coupled to three-axle, 20-tonne Raaymakers drawbar trailers. They were powered by the legendary Gardner

8LW engines, which produced 150bhp. These straight-eight engines were so long that the first 40cm (16in) of the body could not be used. The first part of the body not only accommodated a part of the engine (i.e the last two cylinders), but also some equipment such as shovels and brooms. The first three Haukes Fodens featured in a truck driver's contest that took place in Arnhem in September 1954. One of the photographs show the brand new vehicles in a marketplace that was still surrounded by partly destroyed buildings, eight years after the war had ceased.

In those days Holland already had a very liberal legislation, which allowed operators to use vehicles that

Above: From 1953 onwards Dutch importer Fodenway used these purpose-built premises at Heelsum, a village just west of the city of Arnhem. Fodenway was responsible for the sales and service of Foden trucks in Holland in the 1950s and 1960s, and was closed down in 1965. *(Author's collection)*

could handle gross weights up to 50 tonnes. One of the Haukes drivers told me that its Fodens were regularly grossing at 60 tonnes, which meant that payloads were approaching 40 tonnes. However, with only 150bhp on tap, these vehicles were slow. Very slow. It took ages to get the drawbar outfits up to 40mph and the top speed was about 45mph. Nevertheless, the trucks were very

Above: The headboard of fleet numbers 1, 2 and 3 of the Haukes company told people they were the first four-axle Foden lorries in Holland. The impressive vehicles were fitted with heavy duty steel bumpers incorporating towing pins for positioning the heavy three-axle Raaymakers drawbar trailers. They also had marker sticks fitted to the far ends of the bumper bars, which helped the driver to assess accessibility in restricted areas as the S18 cabs were much narrower than the bodies of both lorries and drawbar trailers. *(Rene Megens collection)*

Below: During weekends and holidays in the 1950s one could watch this impressive line-up of Haukes FG8/15 and FG8/24 brick carriers at their Kekerdom home base. The Haukes company was the biggest Foden customer in Holland operating nineteen Foden brick carriers plus four dump trucks during the 1950s and early 1960s. *(Author's collection)*

strong and reasonably reliable. One of the drawbacks of the S18 cab was that it was very hot in the summer and, due to the absence of a heater, very cold and draughty in the winter. Drivers had to wear leather jackets and gloves, but they still felt the terrible draughts, which came up from the holes in the floor around the clutch and brake pedal.

At the end of the 1950s the Haukes company operated nineteen Foden trucks (seventeen S18s of the FG8/15 and FG8/24 type, two second-hand FG6/12s and one S20 FG6/22). It also operated four FGD6 dump trucks fitted with half cabs, which were used off-road in large sandpits. This made Haukes the biggest Foden operator in Holland.

Above: The first three Foden eight-wheel lorries to be imported into Holland went into service with the Haukes company. The brand new vehicles are seen here at a marketplace in Arnhem in September 1954, competing in a national drivers' contest. This photograph clearly shows that the first 16in of the truck's bodywork was not used for carrying bricks, but to make room for the long eight-cylinder Gardner 8LW. The compartments on the left and right-hand side next to the engine accommodated shovels and brooms. *(Rene Megens collection)*

Left: Haukes fleet number 5 was photographed in front of a typical Dutch windmill in the late 1950s during winter time. The exposed radiator of the FG8/15 model is nearly completely covered by a piece of tarpaulin to keep the engine's cooling water at the right temperature. Driver and mate had to wear thick winter clothes because the S18 cabs had no heaters and the draught from the big holes around the pedals in the cab's floor was immense. PB-36-10 was built and registered in 1954. This image was used to produce a Christmas card in 2006 by Dutchman and Foden enthusiast Rene Megens. *(Rene Megens collection)*

Right: Haukes also operated four FGD6 dump trucks, which were kept busy in large sandpits near the Dutch rivers Rhine and Waal and in Germany. They were powered by Gardner 6LW-112 engines and put into service between 1954 and 1956. This 1955-built FGD6 is finding its way through mud, water and sticky river clay to deliver its heavy load to a brick works. *(Author's collection)*

Other Dutch Operators

There were many other Dutch companies, who also used Fodens. About 80 per cent of the Fodens sold in Holland were used in the brick haulage industry, where they built up quite a reputation within just a few years.

Quite a few operators and lots of drivers did not like the S18 cabs and preferred Dutch coach-built types instead. Some operators did actually replace the cold and draughty S18 cabs by stylish coach-built (sleeper) cabs, or by fitting an existing DAF DO cab. This was done by the Huet company, which owned several Fodens in the 1950s. One of them was a 1955 FG8/24, which transported bricks in the first five years of its life. In 1960 a DAF DO cab replaced the original Foden cab. A tilt body replaced the earlier drop side body to transport crated glass from Germany to Holland.

The Huet company was also the inventor of the Hulo self-loading crane, specially designed for loading and unloading bricks and concrete objects. The first

Below: Most Dutch Fodens were brick carriers, the majority being three- and four-axle drawbar combinations. This two-axle FG5/7.5 model Foden was built in 1948 and despite being fitted with a Gardner 5LW engine, which only produced 85bhp, it pulled a two-axle drawbar trailer to deliver bricks all over the country. It has an elegant Dutch coach-built cab, which provided enough room for driver and mate and the comfort of a heater. The Dutch-built body consists of a steel framework and wooden drop sides. (Author's collection)

ones were introduced in 1960. The cranes became increasingly popular with the brick haulage men. Handballing a drawbar outfit took nearly two hours by two men, so these self-loading cranes made the drivers' life a lot easier than it was before.

Another Huet conversion was a 1957 FGTU6/40 6×4 tractor unit, which was converted into a short wheelbase three-axle rigid. The vehicle was coupled to a three-axle drawbar trailer, which was also fitted with a Hulo self-loading crane. A German GOFA cab replaced the original Foden S18 cab.

In 1955, a brick haulier from Utrecht placed the biggest order ever at Fodenway. He ordered ten Fodens.

Above: Quite a few Dutch operators changed the draughty S18 cabs for coach-built cabs, or in this case an existing DAF 2000DO cab. The massive radiator of the Gardner 8LW, Foden and Gardner badges and the front hubcaps reveal its Foden origin. The 1955 FG8/24 model spent five years of its life carrying bricks and was converted into a covered truck, transporting glass windows, which were unloaded by an adapted Hulo brick crane. (Author's collection)

Six yellow and red FGTU6/30 4×2 tractors, two FG6/24 8×4 rigids and two FG6/14 4×2 rigids were delivered and soon they were hauling bricks to all parts of Holland.

Left: Another Dutch Foden fitted with a coach-built cab is this FGTU6/30 tractor unit and two-axle semi-trailer operated by Baan & Ten Bolscher based in Rijssen, east Holland. It was purchased new in 1955 and was operated for four years on brick haulage. It went to West Germany regularly to deliver bricks in the Harz mountain area. Return cargos were often loads of gypsum building materials. It was powered by a Gardner 6LW engine, which meant that progress in the mountains was slow. *(Author's collection)*

Right: This FGHT6/50 heavy haulage tractor unit was built in 1956. It was originally fitted with a full-width crane carrier type cab, which was derived from the dump truck half cab. Obviously the operators have changed it for a Dutch coach-built cab at some time during its life. The three-axle tractor unit was operated by Niehof Transport based at Rotterdam. It is carrying a heavy piece of machinery, which definitely has an alarming high centre of gravity. *(Niels Jansen collection)*

Above: Another Foden fitted with a Dutch coach-built cab as most drivers did not like the cold and draughty S18 cab. Dutch trailer manufacturer Groenewegen built this special cab for a tipper operator based in the central part of Holland. Groenewegen also manufactured the semi-trailer and tipper body. The FGTU6/40 model was built in 1956 and powered by a Gardner 6LW engine. *(Author's collection)*

Left: Motorways were scarce in Holland in the 1950s and, as can be seen here, almost deserted. It is striking that the left side of the motorway (which was the former two-lane main road) is not constructed in tarmac or in concrete, but still in paving bricks. This FG6/12 model is pulling a three-axle drawbar trailer loaded with 35 tonnes of bricks. It is also striking that an unsecured spare wheel was carried on the back of the trailer! The Gardner 6LW-powered combination was built in 1956. *(Author's collection)*

Left: The driver and owner of this FG8/15 drawbar combination proudly pose for their new brick carrier. Gelsing of Lent, near Nijmegen, were brick merchants. It purchased this truck and drawbar trailer in 1956 but it was only operated until 1958, when the company decided to hand over the transport of bricks to another haulier. It was powered by a Gardner 8LW-150 engine, which could be recognised by its big radiator. *(Armand Bastin collection)*

Above: Weys transport also transported bricks in the 1950s, not only to customers in Holland but also for export to other countries. A 1956 FG6/12 is waiting in front of a customs (Douane) barrier at the Dutch–German border. A Gardner 6LW engine, only producing 112bhp, powered this heavy truck/drawbar trailer combination. The truck was fitted with a Dutch coach-built cab, manufactured by Paul & van Weelde. *(John Sanderson collection)*

Right: Van Huet Bros operated this 1957 FGTU6/40 tractor unit, which is coupled to a purpose-built brick carrying semi-trailer fitted with a Hulo brick crane. The tractor unit was fitted with a German GOFA coach-built cab and was powered by a Gardner 6LW engine, producing a modest 112bhp. The tractor unit was converted into a short wheelbase rigid in the early 1960s. It pulled a three-axle drawbar trailer and Hulo crane to increase payload. *(Author's collection)*

Below: Loading brick carriers with more than 30 tonnes of bricks was a time-consuming job for the driver and his mate, but fortunately other workers also helped out. This FG6/12, built in 1957, is fitted with a British Boalloy aluminium cab. Three men and a boy are loading the vehicle at one of the many brick works, which were built in the water meadows of the big Dutch rivers. *(Author's collection)*

Opposite: Only two of these nice little FE4/8 models were exported to Holland. They had small 2.4-litre four-cylinder Foden FD4 engines, which produced 84bhp. The Van Kooten Brothers operated them for nearly twenty years. This 1956 model carried 8 tons of concrete blocks and was fitted with an aluminium cab. The drop side vehicle is photographed in front of an old Dutch manor called Zonneweelde (Sun wealth) situated in a nice wooded area in central Holland. *(Author's collection)*

Not all Fodens sold in Holland were big and sturdy trucks. Foden also offered the small FE4/8, a nice little truck, powered by Foden's own four cylinder two-stroke engine, which produced a healthy 84bhp. These Fodens had elegant aluminium cabs and, as far as I know, the two vehicles sold in Holland were the only ones that had left-hand drive. They were sold to the Van Kooten Brothers in 1953 and 1956 and gave good service until 1973.

Declining Dutch Sales

At the end of the 1950s Fodens were only sold in low numbers. The new S20 and S21-cabbed Fodens could not compete with the very innovative products of Volvo, Scania–Vabis, Mercedes–Benz and of course, DAF. Only ten Fodens were sold in Holland between 1958 and 1963. Nevertheless, Foden had made its way into Holland and many Fodens had long lives. Most of the Haukes Fodens were kept busy for about ten years and were then replaced by Mack B-series, which became the favourite of the Dutch brick hauliers in the 1960s. Approximately 150 Fodens were sold in Holland between 1948 and 1960, but sadly none of them survived.

British-built trucks became less popular in Holland because the cabs were uncomfortable, sleeper cabs were hardly available and the engines did not have enough power for 50-tonne operations. Finally, the offered engines were not reliable enough. Added to this the after-sales service was weak and in some cases virtually non-existent. That is the main reason why manufacturers such as Foden, Leyland, AEC, Seddon and BMC almost disappeared from the Continental truck markets in the 1960s. Only Bedford survived in Holland and some

Above: This page of a 1960 Dutch Groenewegen brochure shows an early extendable semi-trailer for the transport of long iron bars and rods. The 1957 Foden FGTU6/40 tractor unit was operated by the well-known Dutch heavy haulage company Van der Meijden, which has its base in the western part of Holland, roughly between Amsterdam and The Hague. The Groenewegen CGO24X semi-trailer could handle a payload of 24 tons. Groenewegen also built the roomy sleeper cab, which incorporated the Foden grille panel and logo. *(Author's collection)*

other European countries during the 1970s and early 1980s.

In 1960 the Dutch government needed the premises of Fodenway to build the new A12 motorway to connect the cities of Utrecht and Arnhem. Fodenway was forced to move, but soon found accommodation at a road building and construction company called Bruil. This company already operated a couple of Foden S20 6×4 and 4×2 trucks, which were used as tippers and bulk cement tankers. The Bruil company was in a village called Ede, which was just 8 miles west of the old Fodenway premises.

Owing to the decline of sales in Holland, Foden decided that Fodenway distributors had to close in 1965. However, fortunately Foden did not disappear completely from the Dutch and European truck market.

From 1965 until 1972 it operated Fodens Europe Ltd, which was situated in Lomm near Venlo, a small village in the southern part of Holland near the German border. From there it was able to co-ordinate European sales and distribute Foden parts all over Europe.

Universal

During the 1974 Amsterdam Commercial Vehicle Show, which was held in February, Foden introduced its new Universal chassis. These chassis were specifically designed for Foden's export markets, which allowed higher gross vehicle weights than on the home market. Foden showed a 4×2 tractor chassis, which had a gross combination weight (g.c.w.) of 38 tonnes. The 6×4 tipper chassis had a gross vehicle weight (g.v.w.) of 26 tonnes. Both chassis were powered by a Cummins NTC335 engine. On top of the sturdy Universal tipper chassis, Foden fitted the new steel S90 tilt cab, which was designed and built by Motor Panels of Coventry. The steel cab had a folding glass fibre grille panel. The three-way steel tipper body was manufactured by the well-known German Meiller company. The tractor unit was shown in chassis form to show the neat installation

Below: Foden made a serious attempt to recover a share of the European market in 1974, just after the UK became a member of the European Community. It introduced the Universal range, which consisted of heavy duty export vehicles fitted with Cummins engines and steel S90 cabs. The range was unveiled during the 1974 Amsterdam Show, where a 4×2 tractor unit and a 6×4 tipper were exhibited. The RC33/26 model 26-tonne tipper had a steel three-way tipper body manufactured by the well-known German Meiller company. *(Fodens Ltd)*

of the big 14-litre Cummins engine. The S90 cab could be specified in left- or right-hand drive to meet the requirements of Continental and Middle East markets and operators could also order a sleeper cab version. Production of the Universal range was planned from the autumn of 1974 onwards.

Foden's first targets were the Dutch, Belgium and German markets. At first sight, it seems strange that Foden was attacking the German market, as the Germans usually purchased home-built trucks. But Fodens had just signed an agreement with the German Faun factory, builders of earth moving equipment. Faun and Foden products would be marketed in both the Continental and British markets. Knowing this, Foden's decision made more sense.

Bruil Imports

Bruil was a major road construction company and also a building material merchant. The senior engineer of the Bruil company, Mr van der Vegt, was looking for a couple of heavy four-axle truck chassis for tipper and concrete mixer applications. After visiting the Foden stand at the 1974 Amsterdam Show, the Bruil company was invited to visit the new assembly shop in Sandbach. This resulted in an order for three 8×4 chassis. The trucks would be fitted with S80 cabs, because the S90 versions were not available yet. These chassis were powered by Cummins NH220 engines and fitted with Foden eight-speed gearboxes. In July 1974 the first chassis was exported to Holland, but one of the main problems was getting type approval and so Bruil and Fodens agreed that the first chassis would be supplied on a consignment basis. This meant that the truck remained the property of Foden until the completion of the type approval.

In the meantime Foden had appointed a Dutch agent, who would take care of imports from July 1974 onwards. This company, Geveke of Amsterdam, was also the distributor of Oshkosh and White/Autocar trucks, but the company was also distributing Caterpillar earth moving equipment.

The first Bruil chassis was fitted with a Netam–Fruehauf steel tipper body and after a number of trials the vehicle was type approved in September 1974. Shortly after the first vehicle had hit the road, the other two chassis arrived in Holland. Type approval was already completed, so within a few weeks these chassis were fitted with 8 cu m concrete mixers,

manufactured by Mulder of Boskoop. In November 1974 all three vehicles were put into service. The tipper was painted in Bruil's own colours and both concrete mixers in the colours of EBC, a full subsidiary of Bruil. Within a few months it became clear that the road springs were not heavy enough for a 34-tonne operation, which was 4 tonnes above the design weight. Foden warned Bruil that premature failures due to overloading would not be covered by its warranty terms. Of course, Bruil fitted heavier road springs in order to avoid failures but due to its huge heavy steel body, the tipper was regularly overloaded, which resulted in a few heavy fines. To avoid these,

Left: Bruil's fleet numbers 95 and 96 were put into service in November 1974 after all trials for the Dutch type approval were completed. Both RC22/30 vehicles had Dutch-built Mulder 8 cu m concrete mixers fitted. The vehicles were painted in the colours of Bruil subsidiary EBC, which was the ready mixed concrete branch of this Dutch construction company. Cummins NHK220 engines mated to Foden eight-speed gearboxes powered these impressive and good-looking vehicles. *(Author's collection)*

Right: Bruil purchased another five Fodens in 1975 to shift large amounts of sand for the construction of the new A50 motorway between Zwolle and Apeldoorn in the eastern part of Holland. The FC27A dump trucks were kept very busy for fifteen months. The super single sand tyres on the rear bogie were necessary to keep the vehicles within the deep sand tracks. *(Author's collection)*

Left: An impressive line-up of four Foden FC27As and three Faun articulated dump trucks, which were used for the construction of the A50 motorway. The Bruil company used products of the two companies, which signed an agreement in 1973 to sell and maintain each other's vehicles on the Continent. The big Foden dump trucks had S51 cabs, 310bhp Cummins N855C310 engines and Allison automatic gearboxes. *(Author's collection)*

New Dutch Agent

In the meantime, Foden took part in the 1976 Amsterdam Show, where its Dutch distributor, Geveke, showed the production versions of the Universal chassis, fitted with the S90 cab. First there was a Universal 6×4 tipper chassis, which could be ordered in 26 or 36 tonnes g.v.w. form. The heaviest versions were particularly suitable for off-road purposes in Middle East countries. Cummins NTC 290 or NTC 335 engines powered the Universals. There was also a rigid eight on show, which was derived from the military chassis. This vehicle was powered by a Rolls–Royce Eagle 220 and had a large Mulder of Boskoop 8 cu m concrete mixer on its back.

Unfortunately, Geveke was only able to sell one Foden in Holland in 1976. In the next year the company ceased importing Fodens. The S90 8×4 concrete mixer was eventually sold a few months after the Amsterdam

Below: The Geveke Company, based in Amsterdam, also imported other construction vehicles, as this photograph from 1975 shows clearly. Besides the Foden S80-cabbed RC22/30 tipper it also shows an Autocar 6×6 and an Oshkosh 8×6 tipper chassis. *(Author's collection)*

the company decided to convert the tipper into a concrete mixer in 1977.

All three S80 trucks were sold in 1978 to a Belgium merchant, but after two years all three showed up again in Holland. The vehicles were used for another four to seven years by a small concrete company called Rotink Ltd. It used the parts of two vehicles to keep the last one running.

Bruil purchased another five Fodens in October 1975. They were not normal road going vehicles this time, but genuine off-road FC27A type dumpers. These vehicles were bought in England, through Reg Knowles of Somercote in Derbyshire. Together with three Faun articulated dumpers, all the vehicles were kept very busy for fifteen months constructing part of the new A50 motorway between Zwolle and Apeldoorn in the

eastern part of Holland. Unlike the rest of the country, this consists of woods, heather fields and shifting sand hills. This area is also a little uneven and lots of Dutch people consider these molehills as real hills, although most of the terrain does not exceed 100ft in height.

The FC27As were powered by Cummins N855C310 engines and coupled to Allison automatic gearboxes with torque converters. They could easily maintain a speed of 40 mph off-road while shifting 15 cu m of sand in their huge bodies. The vehicles were fitted with large super single sand tyres on the rear bogie in order to keep track in the big loose sand areas. The Bruil company was very happy with the outstanding performance of the Foden dumpers. As they were far too wide to use on the road, they were sold off to an English merchant when the job was completed, which was in January 1977.

Above: Foden appointed a new Dutch representative in July 1974 to sell the Universal range in Holland. This 32-tonne Foden Universal rigid eight chassis was fitted with a Motor Panels S90 day cab, featuring a full-width windscreen with three wipers and big 11in headlamps. The huge-bonneted Oshkosh is an 8×6 driven tipper powered by a Caterpillar engine. Both vehicles were exhibited in front of the RAI exhibition centre in Amsterdam on a cold winter's day in February 1976. *(Author's collection)*

Right: Another exhibit on Geveke's Foden stand was this very impressive four-axle concrete mixer. The Universal RR22/30 model was derived from the military low mobility chassis, hence the similar front bumper and headlight arrangement. It was fitted with a steel S90 cab and powered by a Rolls–Royce Eagle 220 engine. The 8 cu m concrete mixer was built by the Mulder company, which also sold quite a few mixers to customers in the UK. *(Author's collection)*

Show to a company called Sagro. The owner of this young company only used it for two years, experiencing some serious teething problems such as engine failures. This operator used the Foden demonstrator colours of 1976 (white, blue and yellow) for many years as its company livery.

Dutch Crane Carriers

Foden crane carriers were rare in Holland, but some were operated in the 1970s and 1980s. One of them was owned by a transhipment company, which used this vehicle in harbours all over Holland. Otte Bros of Hillegom imported this vehicle, a four-axle CC 8/12.30 built in 1966, from Ireland in 1978. The vehicle was powered by a Leyland EO 680 engine, which produced 200bhp. However, this engine was soon replaced by the well-known DAF 11.6-litre engine, which produced 230bhp. A heavy Priestman crane was built on the chassis and the whole outfit weighed a staggering 40,000 kilos, which meant that the vehicle was not allowed on the Dutch roads without a special permit. However, provided with a special registration number for mobile cranes (which used to carry ZZ registrations when axle loads and lengths or widths of vehicles were exceeding the maximum values), the vehicle was allowed to use public roads. And it even towed a two-axle drawbar trailer, which carried a small Bobcat shovel and the driver's car! The driver would use his car to get home when a job took more than one day. It saved him the trip home with the heavy and slow Foden and the car was obviously a lot more frugal on fuel. This Foden was operated until well into the 1990s. Otte Bros had bought a second crane carrier from a company in Rotterdam for spares, to keep its own Foden going. The vehicle was still for sale at a Dutch mobile crane merchant in 2003

Right: The Dutch-based Otte Bros operated this Low Line crane carrier during many years. The 1966 model CC8/12.30 chassis was imported from Ireland in 1978. A heavy Priestman crane was fitted to the chassis and the Leyland EO680 engine was replaced by a DAF 11.6-litre engine, producing 230bhp. The whole outfit weighed a stunning 40 tonnes and was operated in many Dutch harbours, transhipping loads from barges to lorries or to quaysides. *(Govert Bouthoorn)*

Above: Another view of the Otte Bros crane carrier when the crane's jib was partly dismantled and the outfit was ready for the next job. Note the Bobcat mini-shovel on the drawbar trailer. *(David Bloor collection)*

Above right: A nice Dutch Foden Low Line crane carrier, which is still operated today. It is an early 1964 model CC8/12.30, now used by a sandblasting company to lift pleasure yachts and small ships from and into the water of the adjacent North Holland canal near Den Helder, an important Dutch naval base. It is fitted with a 27-tonne DEMAG K406T crane. Despite being more than fifty years old, the outfit still looks immaculate. *(Richard Blokker)*

and was eventually exported to India in 2005, being nearly forty years old!

Schiphol Airport Fodens

There were also three or four Fodens working at Schiphol International Airport near Amsterdam in the 1970s and 1980s. BP Air operated these S36 and S81 6×4

heavy tractor units. They were pulling large 80,000-litre tank trailers, which were manufactured by the German Strüver company, based in Hamburg. BP had ordered quite a lot of these trailers, which were big enough to refuel all types of aircraft, including Boeing Jumbo Jets.

BP Air operated these outfits all over Europe at nearly all large airports. Gross combination weights totalled around 100 tonnes. The S36 tractors were powered by Leyland EO690 turbocharged engines. The S81 6×4 tractors were powered by Cummins NH220 engines, which produced enough power to reach a top speed of 25mph. It is obvious that these outfits did not do very high mileages and that is why they lasted for at least fifteen to twenty years. The powerful pumps could discharge the load in less than twenty minutes at 4,500 litres per minute.

Unfortunately, Foden were not able to sell many vehicles in the Dutch or other European markets in the 1960s and 1970s. They were much more successful in the Middle East, South Africa, Australia and a number of Third World countries. Finally, there was one Foden 4000 series operating in Holland in the 1990s, but that is a different story that will be told elsewhere in this book.

Belgium

Early Imports

Foden trucks were sold in Belgium in small quantities during the 1950s and 1960s. Several tractor units and rigid vehicles were sold to small transport companies. During the 1954 Brussels Show (Salon de L'Automobile), which was organised in January, three different Foden models were exhibited in conjunction with Belgian Bus and Truck Co., which was based in Antwerp. Great interest was shown in a rear-engined PVRF6 bus chassis, powered by a Foden FD6 two-stroke engine. There was also a FGTU6/20 tractor unit fitted with a Foden twelve-speed gearbox and the left-hand drive version of the small FE4/8 model. Some crane carrier chassis, bus chassis and aircraft refuellers also found their way to this small country. Despite being a small truck market, one could encounter many British makes in Belgium in the 1950s, 1960s and 1970s.

European Community

As Great Britain became an EC member on 1 January 1973, Foden intended to sell vehicles on the Continental truck market again, starting with Belgium

Right: An early 1960s FC17 crane carrier on one of the many cobbled main roads that were still present in Belgium in the 1960s. The left-hand drive vehicle is being operated by Louis Cop from Awirs near Liege, which is situated in the French-speaking part of the country. It is passing a Caltex fuel station and is being followed by a Volkswagen Transporter Mark 1 and a Belgian-manufactured Auto Miesse articulated tipper combination. It is remarkable that the Ruston's Bucyrus 22RB crane boom is not secured into the well between the two cab parts, but is horizontally facing rearwards without any warning signs for the approaching traffic. Obviously people got away with this in the 1960s. It was quite dangerous and fortunately unheard of nowadays. *(Arthur Ingram).*

and France. The company exhibited a tractor unit
during the Brussels Show in January 1973. The
vehicle, a model 4AR6/34, fitted with an S80 day
cab was powered by a Rolls–Royce Eagle Mark II
engine, producing 220hp. It was coupled to a Foden
nine-speed gearbox. The Brussels-based Novarobel
company was appointed as the Belgium agent. As
the vehicle was based on British specifications with a
design gross combination weight of only 34 tons and
the glass fibre S80 cab was only available in day cab
form, this attempt to conquer the Belgian market was
not a success, to put it mildly.

4000 Series

After its failure in the 1970s, Foden made another
attempt to conquer the Belgian market in 1990 by
appointing Cummins Distributors Belgium (CDB) as
Foden agents in Brussels. The successful 4000 series
introduced in Great Britain in 1987 and Paccar decided
the time was right to sell these vehicles on the European
market. The first left-hand drive 4000 series, a 4×2
tractor unit, was delivered to CDB at the beginning of
1990.

In January 1991 CDB was present during the Brussels
Show, introducing a 4000 series 4×2 tractor unit fitted
with the new Hi-Line sleeper cab. The launch of this
high-roof sleeper cab was targeted at the long distance
operator involved in European transport. It provided
interior headroom of up to 1.8m and became available
in single and double bunk versions. In comparison
with the single bunk sleeper cab, the new cab gave the
driver 350mm more headroom. The show vehicle was
fitted with a Cummins NTAA465 engine and had a
design gross combination weight of 48 tonnes. It was

obvious that Foden had not made the same mistake
as in 1973 because this vehicle was fully adapted to
Continental legislation and operators' requirements.
The second vehicle on show was an 8×4 chassis, fitted
with a Cummins NTE320 engine. It had Kenworth
KW6/50A rear suspension, which created a greater
ground clearance. This vehicle could operate in Belgium

at 32 tonnes gross weight. As the chassis and cab weight
was 9.4 tonnes, it allowed a body and payload of 22.6
tonnes.

Belgium Sales

Some British commercial vehicle journalists wondered why Paccar was so anxious to enter the European truck market again. They were not sure whether Foden could be sold in significant figures in Europe. They were dead right – selling Fodens in the European market turned out to be a low volume job and Belgium was no exception. Only twelve vehicles were sold in Belgium during the 1990s. Eleven were 4×2 tractor units and only one 8×4 chassis hit the Belgium roads. As CDB was also the Cummins importer for Belgium it is no surprise that Cummins engines powered most of the vehicles, but some had Caterpillar 3406B-350 engines. One of these Caterpillar-powered S104T-4350 tractor units entered service with the Caterpillar organisation. It pulled a three-axle exhibition semi-trailer, which was operated in all parts of Europe, including Russia.

Below: Herreman Transport of Wevelgem used this Cat-powered Foden for pulling sea containers into and out of the ports of Antwerp and Zeebrugge. It was powered by a reliable and strong 3406B-425 engine and fitted with the wedge-shaped 4000 series sleeper cab. It is striking that is has a British flag painted on the front bumper, probably to let people know the driver is using a British-built truck. *(Author's collection)*

Left: The Caterpillar organisation operated this 1991 Belgian-registered model pulling an exhibition trailer. It went to all parts of Europe including Russia, hence the Cyrillic lettering that can be seen on the sides of the semi-trailer. The S104T-4350 was, of course, powered by a Cat engine, the 3406ATAAC producing 350bhp. *(Author's collection)*

Right: Another Belgian haulier that operated a Foden was Piron Transport. This S104T-4350 model 4×2 tractor unit was purchased in 1994. The vehicle was photographed along the E19 motorway between Antwerp and Brussels in 1996. It was fitted with a Hi-Line sleeper cab and powered by a Caterpillar 3406B-350 engine. Piron operated more "exotic" vehicles, such as Spanish Pegasos. The Foden pulls an Italian intermodal tilt trailer. *(Leo Jacobse)*

After a couple of years CDB ceased importing Foden vehicles. A company called Eurocamions did the servicing of the remaining Belgium Fodens. Eurocamions even owned an impressive S104T-4500 tractor powered by a Cummins N500E engine and fitted with the Hi-Line cab, which it rented out to customers. Eurocamions ceased trading in 2004.

France

Early Exports

Exports to France never reached significant numbers. This is most likely caused by the fact that the French always have had a robust commercial vehicle industry of their own. Nevertheless, George Milhommes, who was Foden's agent in Paris, serviced about thirty war-type DG6/10 six-wheelers for many years, well into the 1950s. These vehicles had been left behind in France after World War II and were operated by hauliers based near and in Paris. Apart from the numerous Foden aircraft refuellers that were operating at important French airfields, only a few vehicles were sold to French companies in the last fifty years.

The most impressive vehicles sold to a French company were two heavy haulage tractors, which were purchased by Le Materiel Electrique from Paris in 1961. These FCHT6/80 double drive ballasted tractors were sent to Malaysia to move heavy transformers and other equipment to a hydroelectric power station in the Cameron Highlands. The vehicles were powered by Cummins NH220 engines and had twelve-speed Foden gearboxes. The chassis were equipped with S20 day cabs, which had double-skinned tropical roofs. The ballast boxes contained 20 tons of cast iron and both vehicles were equipped with Darlington rear winches. They were also provided with radio communication equipment to guarantee first class communication between the two drivers and the trailer steersman. The six-axle Crane drawbar girder trailer could be extended to 57ft and had a designed payload of a little over 70 tons. It had two automatically steered bogies, each fitted with three axle rows. Including the pushing Foden, the whole outfit measured 120ft.

Above: Air BP purchased lots of "Cornwall" aircraft refuellers in the 1950s, which were put into service at airfields all around the world. Quite a few were operated at the Paris Orly and Le Bourget airports for many years. They were transferred to smaller airports later, like this 1956 FG6/20 model that was photographed at a small French airport in 1979. The vehicle still looked well maintained despite being twenty-three years old. *(Author's collection)*

Right: These two FCHT6/80 ballast tractors were owned by a Paris-based company that exported transformers to all parts of the world. It is seen here in the Malaysian Cameron Highlands, negotiating a tight bend, one Foden pulling and the other pushing. The Cummins NH220-powered vehicles had Foden twelve-speed gearboxes and pulled/pushed a 70-ton capacity Crane girder trailer featuring six axle rows. Both vehicles were built in 1961 and put into service the next year. Gross weight of this impressive heavy haulage combination was a staggering 160 tons. *(Author's collection)*

Gross combination weight reached a figure of around 160 tons.

4000 series

Although Foden tried to gain a part of the French truck market by showing its Universal series at the 1974 Paris Show, it took until the early 1990s before new Fodens could be seen on French roads. The Navi Norpen company, situated in a village near Lille, was appointed Foden's sole dealer in France in 1989. This company also imported Kenworth trucks that were put into operation with its sister company, Transports Wauthier. It was no surprise that most of the imported Fodens also worked for Transports Wauthier. The first Foden, a S106T-4450 double drive tractor unit, was powered with a top of the range Caterpillar 3406B engine, producing 425bhp. It could operate at 44 tonnes gross.

Below: The French Navi Norpen company was the Paccar importer and sold Kenworths, Peterbilts and Fodens in France. Some of the 4000 series Fodens worked for a sister company called Wauthier, based in Carvin, including this 1989 S106T-4300, which was powered by a Caterpillar 3306ATAAC-300 engine. (*Author's collection*)

Left: A S106T double drive tractor unit pulling a Debeaux tank semi-trailer. It dates from around 1990 but as it has no model badge it could be powered by a big Cat 3406B-350 or 425 engine, or a Cummins NTE350/400. The truck was registered in the Somme district, not far from the Foden importer's base at Lille. It was photographed in June 1992 at the Van Ommeren Matex terminal in the Rotterdam harbour area. *(Lex Meeder)*

Right: BOC purchased eight 4000-series 4×2 tractor units in 1991, servicing the prestigious Marks & Spencer contract to supply its Paris store. Four of them were ordered in right-hand drive and were registered in the UK. The other four were left-hand drive models registered in France and operated by BOC Transvite (French for fast transport). All eight vehicles were powered by Cummins NTE365 engines. Return cargoes to the UK were collected in Spain and Italy and these could be perfume, hanging garments or flowers. *(Author's collection)*

Opposite: TRPM, based in the Strasbourg area, operated this nice S104T-4450 tractor unit from 1992. It is fitted with the wedge-shaped sleeper cab. The 4×2 tractor unit was powered by a Caterpillar 3406B-425 engine and pulls a curtain-sided semi-trailer in the livery of GEBO Industries, a foodstuffs company from Reichstett near the German border. *(Author's collection)*

Below: A partly dismantled Foden steamer is craned off a flatbed railway wagon at a Spanish railway station, probably around 1920. It is very likely that this is a refurbished steamer that was used in World War I in France. *(David Bloor collection)*

Other French Fodens were sold in the popular 4×2 tractor unit configuration. BOC Distribution Services ordered four left-hand drive S104T-4400 Hi-Line 4×2 tractor units for deliveries to the Paris-based Marks & Spencer store. The Cummins NTE365-powered, French-registered Fodens were painted in BOC Transvite livery. The vehicles operated with new 13.6m enclosed semi-trailers, which could take twenty-six pallets.

Spain

Some truck chassis, airfield refuellers, crane carriers and quite a few dump trucks were sold in Spain in the 1950s, 1960s and 1970s. At the end of the 1950s, one or two FG6/14 truck chassis were converted into coaches. The Spanish agent from Madrid exhibited Foden products during several Barcelona Trade Fairs in the 1950s and early 1960s and a long wheelbase S20 eight-wheeler

Left: These Foden DG-series were exhibited during the Valencia Fair at the end of the 1940s. The Fodens were announced as "Camiones Ingleses" (English trucks). The heavy 6×4 tipper in the foreground is a DG6/12 chassis fitted with a drop side steel tipper body. The photograph was taken by the Spanish photographer Gabrelles Siguenza. *(John Sanderson collection)*

Right: A 1952 rear-engined PVRF6 Foden coach, ex-Global Tours of London, appeared in the Spanish Canary Islands late in the 1950s. It had a Metalcraft body and was operated until the late 1960s by the La Tropical brewery, based in the island of Gran Canaria, for the transportation of its employees. *(David Bloor collection)*

Left: Padrosa of Figueres (Catalunya) operated this 1991 high roof S104T-4450 model. The Foden was probably a trial vehicle in an Iveco-dominated fleet. It had a powerful Caterpillar 3406B engine, which produced 425bhp. Nowadays, Padrosa specialises in domestic and eastern European freight services. It operates a fleet of 150 trucks and more than 300 curtain-siders, box trailers and low-loaders. *(Author's collection)*

Right: At least two Fodens were operated in the Spanish Canary Islands and this S106T-4450 tipper combination worked on the mountainous island of La Palma. A Caterpillar 3406B-425 engine provided ample power for work in difficult conditions. It was photographed in 1994, when the vehicle was just three years old. The other Foden was based on Tenerife and pulled a three-axle refrigerated semi-trailer. *(Leonard Looijenga)*

in the Canary Islands. Foden 4000 series were exported to Spain in small numbers in 4×2 and 6×4 tractor unit configurations.

Switzerland

Friderici Connection

Apart from some crane carriers and one or two dump trucks, Foden had not sold many vehicles to Switzerland until a large transport company was appointed Foden's Swiss agent in 1990. Friderici SA (Ltd) based in Tolochenaz near Lausanne at the borders of Lake Geneva, had been renowned for operating "exotic" Kenworth trucks since the 1970s. The Friderici transport company was established in 1890 to collect wine casks from vineyards in the area. In 1990 it operated nearly 220 trucks and had a workforce of around 350. It also branched out in warehousing. Although the wine haulage was still an important activity of Friderici in the 1990s, it also transported many other commodities all over Switzerland and abroad. National haulage is its core business as about two-thirds of the vehicles are busy within Switzerland.

Sandbach Visit

When Foden became a member of the Paccar Group in 1980, it was keen to expand into Europe. As Friderici already used Paccar products, Foden asked managing director Jean-Paul Friderici to try one of its products. At first Mr Friderici was not very keen to buy British products, but that changed completely after a visit to the Sandbach factory in 1990. The Friderici people watched

and a heavy 6×4 dump truck were exhibited during the 1959 fair. During the fair, negotiations with a Spanish contractor consortium resulted in an order for twenty dump trucks. The vehicles would be put into service with a major Barcelona harbour project.

At the time, Foden dump trucks were being used for harbour extensions, dam constructions, opencast mines and hydroelectric schemes at Cadiz, Almaraz and in the Grenada area. In 1957 Hidro-electrica Espanola SA of Madrid operated six FRD6 dump trucks during the construction of a dam near Trujillo, about 120 miles south-west of Madrid.

In the late 1950s a 1952 rear-engined PVRF6 Foden coach, fitted with a Metalcraft body, appeared in the Spanish Canary Islands. Previously it had done many Continental trips for the well-known British-based Global Tours. It was operated by the La Tropical

brewery for the transportation of its employees until the late 1960s.

It took until the late 1980s before more Fodens went to Spain. In 1989 the Madrid-based IVISA company was appointed Foden's Spanish main dealer to sell 4000 series vehicles. Its parent company was a major supplier of truck parts to the Spanish commercial vehicle market. The first sales consisted of a 4×2 tractor unit powered by a Caterpillar engine and a 6×4 heavy haulage tractor unit for 70-tonne operations.

In 1991 IVISA took part in the Barcelona Trade Fair by showing a 4000 series 4×2 tractor unit powered by a Caterpillar 3406B – 425bhp engine, coupled to an Eaton thirteen-speed transmission. The left-hand drive tractor unit was fitted with a Hi-Line double bunk sleeper cab and could operate at 40 tonnes. In the same year three new sub-dealers were appointed, including one

Left: The 32-ton FGD series dump truck on the left was exported to a construction equipment merchant in Villeneuve, Switzerland. The 30-ton capacity Low Line crane carrier on the right was sold to the German crane builder DEMAG, based in Dusseldorf. Both vehicles were driven overland in 1964 to their new owners. They took the Felixstowe–Rotterdam ferry and were fitted with signs in the Dutch language on the front, which told people that these vehicles were dangerous and wide. *(David Bloor collection)*

Right: One of the very few Fodens that entered Switzerland before 1990 was this Low Line crane carrier, which was fitted with a Jones crane. The CC8-12/30 crane carrier dates from around 1969. It is working on an avalanche protection gallery, which is a very common protection facility for motorists in Switzerland. *(Author's collection)*

how Fodens were built and were very impressed. They noticed that Fodens were built the American way by using many lightweight components. The vehicles could also be painted in Friderici's striking livery on Foden's assembly lines. Caterpillar engines, composite cabs and Peterbilt-designed Air-Trac suspensions were other features that were very attractive to the Swiss. One has to bear in mind that Swiss legislation only allowed 28-tonne gross combination weights within the country at the time. There was an exception for vehicles entering or leaving Switzerland from places close to the borders; they were allowed to gross at 40 tonnes. So, it was not entirely a surprise that Friderici was appointed as Foden's agent in Switzerland.

First Trucks

Four different Fodens were delivered to Friderici towards the end of 1990. The batch consisted of a 4×2, 6×4 and 8×4 rigid vehicle and a 4×2 tractor unit

Below: One of the first trucks entering the Friderici fleet was this 28-tonne S104T-4450 model. Fleet number 212 was built in 1990 and had a very powerful Caterpillar 3406B-425 engine fitted to conquer the Swiss mountain roads. As it was used for domestic traffic it grossed at only 28 tonnes, hence the two-axle semi-trailer that was used for a Coca-Cola contract. *(Niels Jansen)*

that had to complete Swiss-type approval tests. The rigid vehicles would pull drawbar trailers in various configurations. All were fitted with high-power Caterpillar 3406B engines, which produced 425bhp. Non-synchromesh thirteen-speed Eaton RTO 15613A gearboxes were coupled to the engines. They were also equipped with Voith VR130 hydraulic retarders and Peterbilt air suspension for safe operations on the steep Swiss mountain roads. Friderici chose 4000 series high roof cabs fitted with double bunks to keep the drivers happy, as they were used to big Kenworth K100s fitted with Aerodyne cabs. The fully equipped sleeper cab 4×2 tractor unit only weighed 7,300kg, including 400 litres of fuel.

Big Order

After completing type approval, Friderici ordered no fewer than thirty-two Fodens, which were delivered in 1991. This batch consisted of sixteen tractor units in 4×2 configuration (model S104T-4450) for domestic 28-tonne operations. Eleven 6×4 (model S106R-4450), four 8×4 (model S108-4450) and one 4×2 (model S104R-4450) drawbar outfits completed the order.

Above: Some three-axle Friderici chassis were fitted with tanker bodies, including this 1991 S106R-4450 model. Fleet number 153 has just uncoupled its drawbar trailer and is nearly ready to be loaded with another load of wine. Friderici's fleet numbers consist of the last two or three digits in its registration number, which in this case is VD8153. *(Author's collection)*

Left: Foden received a repeat order from Friderici in 1993, which all had S10 Mark 4 Hi-Line day- or sleeper cabs fitted, featuring the restyled grille panel. This Caterpillar 3406B-400-powered S108R4-4400 model was brand new when photographed in Friderici's yard in Tolochenaz on the edge of Lake Geneva in early 1994. The four-axle chassis had an aluminium tipper body fitted. Although not having a registration plate yet, the registration number must have been allocated already as the vehicle shows its fleet number, 144. *(Author's collection)*

33

Opposite: Eleven of the thirty-two Foden vehicles ordered by Friderici in 1991 had the six-wheel configuration. They were mainly used for international transport, which permitted much higher gross weights than in Switzerland. Quite a few had tilt bodies and pulled two-axle drawbar trailers. All Friderici vehicles ordered in 1991 were equipped with Caterpillar 3406B-425 engines, high roof S10 Mark 4 cabs and aluminium fuel tanks and wheels. *(Niels Jansen)*

Below: This wine tanker is also fitted with the 4000-series Mark 4 Hi Line cab and dates from 1993. Fleet number 81 is an S104T4-4400 model, powered by a Caterpillar 3406B-400 engine. *(Author's collection)*

Left: Another impressive shot of the same vehicle crossing a ford in Mongolia. *(Globetrucker organisation)*

Opposite: Globetrucker is a Swiss charity organisation that delivers school equipment and teaching materials to developing countries in eastern parts of Asia. Founder Yves Ballenegger piloted an ex-Friderici (fleet number 30) Foden during Globetrucker's first trip to Mongolia. It was a 20,000km round trip that started in July 2003 and was completed towards the end of that year after an eventful voyage through many countries in Asia and Europe. The Caterpillar 3406B-425-engined S106R-4450 model, dating from 1991, provided ample power and is seen here on a narrow dirt track among astonishing Mongolian scenery. *(Globetrucker organisation)*

Right: Globetrucker did another two trips to Asia in 2004, one to Vladivostok and another to Mongolia. Both truck and drawbar trailer (18.75m long in total) are equipped with demountable containers. An additional living compartment has been added behind the cab and is equipped with a kitchen, shower, bed and storage room. VD1230 is seen here on a wet day on its way to Vladivostok, the most eastern harbour town in the former USSR. This adventurous voyage involved a distance of 27,000km. *(Globetrucker organisation)*

Swiss Road Test

Friderici soon became the biggest Foden operator on the Continent. Its vehicles became a regular sight in Switzerland and abroad and helped Foden to increase exports into Europe. The trade press reported regularly on these magnificent looking vehicles. *Swiss Camion* (Truck) magazine did a road test with one of the first S104T-4450 4×2 tractor units in 1991. It concluded that the vehicle had many plus points such as the very low weight, caused by the use of many light components such as aluminium fuel tanks and chassis cross members. The composite cab also contributed to this low weight. Despite producing 425bhp, and what is more important, lots of torque (1,966Nm at only 1,200rpm), the Caterpillar engine used only 35 litres of diesel on every 100km. Only a few minor features were not very well liked by the testers, such as no electric windows, a very loud indicator noise and a co-driver's seat that had no suspension.

Geneva Show

In January 1992, Foden took part in the Geneva Show for the first time by exhibiting two models. The first exhibit was a 4×2 tractor unit, fitted with the new Hi-Line cab and powered by a Perkins TX375 engine. The 8×4 rigid for 28-tonne operation in Switzerland was powered by a Caterpillar 3406B-425 engine and equipped with a Voith VR130 retarder, which provided 3,000Nm of braking power. The rigid eight had the old type, high roof, sleeper cab fitted and was liveried in Friderici colours.

Other Swiss Fodens

Contractors in the construction industry operated some Foden CC-type crane carriers in Switzerland in the 1960s. Friderici purchased its Fodens mainly for its own transport business, but it also sold a few to other Swiss operators. The most impressive vehicle was a 6×4 tractor unit (model S106T-4450) fitted with the double bunk Hi-Line cab. The chassis was tailored for logging operations and featured a chassis-mounted Epsilon loading crane. The Caterpillar 3406B-425-powered

Above: After many years working for Friderici this 1991 high roof tractor unit was sold to a Swiss showman. The Globetrucker organisation purchased it to organise another relief operation to Mongolia in 2007. The S104T-4450 tractor unit was eventually sold to a Mongolian operator, which used it for local transport in and around the capital of Ulaanbataar, which has a population of more than a million people. The Cat 3406B-425 powered vehicle pulls a Fruehauf two-axle tilt trailer and is piloted by a Mongolian driver. *(Yves Ballenegger)*

The rigids were mainly used for international haulage at 40 tonnes gross weight, such as hauling wine from Spain and Italy. All vehicles had the same specifications as the first four test vehicles. Most tractor units pulled two-axle trailers fitted with tautliner bodies. The rigids had tilt or tank bodies fitted and most pulled two-axle drawbar trailers, some of them in mid-axle configuration. In 1993–94 Friderici ordered a few more Fodens, which all had the new Hi-Line cab fitted. Power came from 400bhp Caterpillar 3406B engines. The repeat order comprised some 4×2 tractor units (model S104T4-4400) and one or two tipper chassis (model S108R4-4400).

Above: Salamin Freres (Bros) of Chalais was another Swiss operator, which purchased a heavy duty 6×4 tractor unit in 1991. The left-hand drive chassis was specially suited for logging operations, featuring an Epsilon timber crane that had not been mounted yet when the vehicle was photographed at Sandbach prior to delivery. The chassis featured a S10 Mark 4 double bunk Hi-Line cab fitted with a massive protection bar, double air horns and a set of flashing beacons. *(Foden Trucks)*

vehicle was delivered to the Salamin Brothers in Chalais. The Swiss logs were mainly destined for Italy. Apart from this striking vehicle, only one or two 4000 series tractor units were sold to other Swiss operators.

Portugal

Munhas Limitada

Great Britain has always had a good economic relationship with Portugal; you only have to think of the wine trade and in particular the port that has been shipped for centuries from Portugal to Great Britain. As many British merchants were involved in this business, opportunities for other businesses also arose.

In 1949 Munhas Limitada, based in Lisbon, was appointed the official agent for Foden vehicles in Portugal and the Portuguese West African colonies, such as Angola. Managing Director Joaquim Ramos Munha founded the company in 1925. It was agreed that Munhas Ltd would sell a comprehensive range of Foden vehicles, including bus and coach chassis. Most chassis were sent to Portugal in c.k.d. form and built up at the Munhas workshops, which were based near the Lisbon docks. The company also manufactured coach-built cabs and bodies. At the same time a sales and service department was set up in Lisbon's prestigious Avenida da Liberdade.

Mr Munha frequently visited the Foden works in Sandbach in the 1950s. His eldest son, Jose Munha, was sent to Sandbach in order to gain experience in manufacture and maintenance methods. After his seven-month stay in Sandbach he moved on to Paticroft (Manchester) to get some more experience at Gardners.

Poden

As the Portuguese word *foder* (equivalent to an English four-letter word) was spelt nearly the same as Foden, it was understandable that Munhas did not want to market Foden vehicles under their own name. Much to Foden's embarrassment, this language problem was found out at the last moment, just before the delivery of

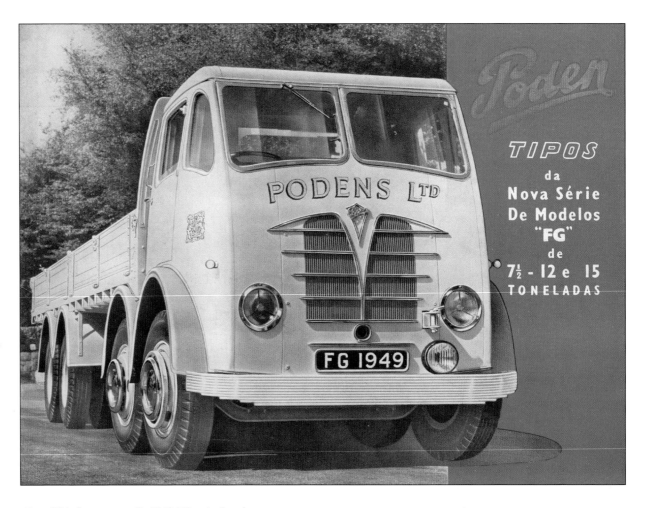

Above: This front cover of a 1949 FG-series brochure clearly shows the Poden name and logo. It saved the Foden management the embarrassment of selling its products under the Foden name as in Portuguese it was very similar to an infamous English four-letter word. *(John Sanderson collection)*

the first vehicles. It was decided that Portuguese Foden vehicles would be marketed as Poden. As the letter F in the Foden logo could easily be changed into a P, this potentially painful problem was solved quickly.

Portuguese Sales in the 1950s

Many Poden trucks found their way to Portuguese operators in the 1950s. In those days 4×2 and 6×4 rigid chassis were the most popular vehicles in Portugal. Many had drop side bodies and coach-built cabs produced by Munhas. That is why many of the 1950s Portuguese Fodens had beautifully styled cabs, incorporating the Poden logo and in many cases the S18 grille panel. A few Poden coach and bus chassis were sold to small Portuguese operators. A company based in Carnaxide near Lisbon took delivery of three right-hand drive PVSC6 bus chassis between 1952 and 1955. More than

Right: This is a long wheelbase Poden FG dating from the early 1950s. It is fitted with an elegant Portuguese coach-built cab. In most cases cabs and bodies were built by importer Munhas Limitada, which was based in Lisbon. *(John Sanderson collection)*

Right: Viacao Mecanica of Carnaxide near Lisbon operated several Poden passenger vehicles in bus and coach form. This PVSC6, dating from 1953, is fitted with a flamboyant Caetano body. More than twenty years later these vehicles were still operated, although their bodies had been replaced by new ones in the mid-1960s. All three had clocked up more than a million kilometres by then. A front-mounted Gardner 6LW-112bhp engine powered this remarkable vehicle. *(Author's collection)*

twenty years later they were still operated by the same company, although they all received replacement bodies in the mid-1960s to make them look more modern.

More Podens in the 1960s

Munhas Ltd regularly exhibited Poden products at the Lisbon International Fair. Various Poden models were on show, including the popular dump truck range.

These fairs attracted a lot of Poden customers and even the Portuguese prime minister paid a visit to the Munhas stand.

Heavy haulage models were also sold in small numbers. The Da Silva company based in Matosinhos near Oporto operated a 6×4 FETU6/72 tractor unit, which was coupled to a 50-ton Dyson two-axle low-loader. The heavy Poden fitted with a coach-built cab was powered by a Foden FD6 Mark 7 two-stroke engine,

Above: This PVRG6 model, powered by a rear-mounted Gardner 6LW engine, was also delivered to Viacao Mecanica of Carnaxide. The coach was built in 1952 and had its old body changed by a more modern Portuguese Caetano body in the mid-1960s. It was eventually operated for more than twenty years until the early 1970s. *(Peter Tulloch collection).*

Left: Heavy haulage specialist Goncalo da Silva of Matosinhos, near Oporto, took delivery of this heavy tractor unit in 1963. The FETU6/72 model was powered by a Foden FD6 Mark 7 two-stroke engine, developing 225bhp coupled to a twelve-speed Foden gearbox. It had a coach-built cab fitted and normally pulled a 50-ton capacity Dyson low-loader, which is shown here. *(John Sanderson collection)*

Right: The same heavy haulage tractor operated by Goncalo da Silva, but now in ballasted form. The ballast existed of heavy wooden beams, which were tied down to the body. The big vessel on the two seven-axle platform trailers weighed 118 tons and was 38m long. Gross combination weight of the whole outfit was 174 tons. The vessel was transported from the Leixoes harbour to the Sacor oil refinery in Oporto, a distance of only 2 miles. A policeman on his bicycle (behind the trailers) formed the legal escort during these trips, which tells all about the speed that was achieved. *(David Bloor collection)*

EXPORTS EUROPE _____

Above: This late 1960s Gardner-powered 4X6/16 chassis has been fitted with a beautiful Portuguese coach-built cab, which clearly shows the large Poden lettering. It was operated by Camionagem Moderna de Fafe Lda for moving general cargo. *(David Bloor collection)*

Left: Another Poden fitted with a typical Portuguese coach-built cab. It was built on a late 1960s left-hand drive 6X6/22 chassis, which was powered by a Gardner 6LX-150 engine. It has a drop side body with only two side boards. It was operated by Transportes Damasio, Joao Lopes Bexiga & Ca Lda of Lisbon on the Lisbon–Alhandra route. *(David Bloor collection)*

which produced 225bhp. It was also used regularly as a ballasted tractor unit, pulling two independent trailers to move large indivisible loads weighing up to 175 tons. The outfit's gross combination weight was a staggering 256 tons. A S41 model 6×4 heavy haulage tractor unit later replaced this vehicle. A Cummins NTK270 engine coupled to a Foden twelve-speed gearbox powered this 200-ton plus vehicle. Towards the end of the 1960s a new agent, Enromotal of Lisbon, was appointed to represent Foden's products in Portugal.

Enromotal and Blandy Bros

Enromotal continued selling Podens in Portugal in the 1970s. It also exhibited Podens regularly at the Lisbon International Trade Fair. Most Podens still had coach-built cabs and drop side bodies, but tractor units became more popular later.

Another Portuguese company, Blandy Brothers, also based in Lisbon, was appointed Foden's dump truck agent for Portugal and it sold dump trucks to quarries and cement works in several parts of Portugal. The CIBRA cement plant of Leiria took delivery of two FC17 dump trucks fitted with the old type half cab in 1974. The vehicles were used to transport cement over

Above: Dating from the early 1970s, this 4AX6/41 model was fitted with a coach-built cab by Salvador Caetano from Oporto. It was one of several Fodens operated by Esso Standard Portuguesa at Lisbon Airport. It was powered by a Gardner 6LX-150 engine coupled to a Foden twelve-speed gearbox and could handle gross weights of 41 tons. *(Julian Hollinshead collection)*

Right: Bearing the Poden badge, it is quite clear that this 1971 heavy duty tractor unit is destined for Portugal. It was fitted with a steel S41 day cab and had a heavy towing pin incorporated into the front bumper. The left-hand drive 6AC6/44 model could gross at 44 tons and was standard fitted with a Cummins NHK205B engine, while a NHK250B was optional. *(John Sanderson collection)*

Above: Goncalo da Silva of Matosinhos replaced the two-stroke-powered Poden with a Cummins-powered 6×4 tractor unit, which was fitted with a S41 steel (Motor Panels) cab in around 1974. The new tractor could also be used in ballast form, as this photograph shows. It pulled an Italian-built Cometto 5+5 girder trailer, which was loaded with an 80-ton transformer that had to be moved from Oporto to the Algarve in southern Portugal. Gross combination weight, including a 30-ton ballast weight, was 200 tons. The journey of 470 miles took sixteen days and was escorted by two policemen. Average speed was a modest 4 miles per hour. The left-hand drive Poden was powered by a Cummins NTK270 engine, coupled to a Foden twelve-speed gearbox. *(David Bloor collection)*

bad service roads from the quarry to the nearby cement processing plant.

Poden imports ceased towards the end of the 1970s, when Foden went into receivership and was finally taken over by the American Paccar group. Enromotal was still representing Foden during the 1990s to provide Portuguese Poden lorry and marine engine operators with the necessary parts.

Greece

Successful Greek Agent

Although Foden had had several agents in Greece during the 1950s and 1960s, sales in that part of Europe were not particularly successful. However, that changed in 1970 when Chryssafis Trading in Athens was appointed as a Foden agent. Mr J.E. Foden went to Athens to

Below: This 6AX6/40 model 6×4 tractor unit was built in 1964 and fitted with an export type S21 cab, featuring an insulated double roof cab. The Greek operator also ordered a Hands (Letchworth) UTSK 20-ton tipper trailer, fitted with a lightweight suspension and an all steel tipper body. An independent, petrol-engined driven pump powered the twin front-end tipping rams. *(Author's collection)*

visit the new agent in the same year. Mr Chryssafis, described as a dynamic businessman, had invited many quarry owners to demonstrate Foden's highly successful range of dump trucks for the event.

Britannia

The demonstrations coincided with the arrival of a Foden C-type steamer, called *Britannia*. The steamer had started a global tour, sponsored by Britannia Electronics, from the Earls Court Motor Show in London on 15 October 1969. The crew, two young men and two even younger women, crossed Belgium, Holland, Germany, Luxembourg, France, Italy and Yugoslavia before they

Below: A fully restored 1926 Foden C-type steamer started a trip around the world in 1969. Foden was one of the sponsors and used the vehicle and crew regularly for publicity purposes. The steamer is seen here in front of the famous Acropolis mountain in Athens with the Parthenon in the background. Two bright yellow Greek Foden dump trucks in the Greek importer's livery were also exhibited in this nice Greek setting in February 1970. *(Author's collection)*

reached the Greek capital on 9 February 1970. The 6-ton overtype Foden steamer dated from 1926 and developed 49bhp. It was fully restored in the year prior to the tour. It was expected to travel 22,500 miles over land and 11,800 miles by sea. The trip would take nearly two years to complete. Of course, Foden was most happy to use the old steamer for publicity purposes. It was parked between a couple of bright yellow Foden dump trucks in front of the famous Acropolis in Athens. The next stop for the steamer was Ankara in Turkey. From there it travelled through countries such as Iran, Afghanistan and Pakistan to India, from where it was shipped to Australia. In December 1971 it was shipped to the United States, where it arrived at San Francisco. After a trip across the USA, WL916 ended her Global Tour in Jacksonville, Florida, in the summer of 1973, nearly four years after she had left Great Britain.

Greek Sales

As Chryssafis was also an agent for Winget concrete mixer drums, the Greek agent sold several Foden 6×4 concrete mixer chassis fitted with S50 type half cabs.

However, the 8×4 chassis were also popular, particularly as long wheelbase heavy duty tippers. They were fitted with S40 or S41 steel cabs and powered by Cummins NHK250 engines, while later models had Cummins NTC335 turbo engines. Some of them operated in quarries at 45 tons gross vehicle weight, which resulted in 30-ton payloads. The agent also sold a few 6×4 heavy haulage tractors, fitted with S41 steel cabs. Finally, Foden FC type 4×2 and 6×4 dump trucks were sold to at least eight Greek quarry owners.

Apart from the words Foden and Cummins, which obviously could not be translated, Greek Foden brochures were printed in Greek characters, which were hard to understand for other people! Chryssafis was the Foden agent until 1977, when another Greek

Below: Greek operators favoured long wheelbase Foden chassis for concrete mixer and tipper operations. This 8XB6/30 model was delivered to the Greek importer in around 1972. The right-hand drive 30-ton tipper chassis featured a S40 day cab and could be powered by either a Gardner 6LXB-180 or a Cummins NHK250 engine. The vehicle is photographed outside the importer's premises in Athens. *(Author's collection)*

company in Athens, Tsekouras SA, took over. It is not known how many Fodens the latter company sold in the following years until the Paccar takeover in 1980 but it is not thought to be many.

Ireland

Early Sales

Foden sales can be traced back to the establishment of the Irish Republic in 1921. At least six C-type steamers fitted with drop side bodies were operated by the Merchants Warehousing Co. Ltd in Dublin in the 1920s. A letter from the managing director in an old brochure states that Foden steamers were quite frugal on coal in comparison with their competitors. Engines and boilers were also easy to clean and to work on in the event of repairs.

Dublin based W.F. Poole & Co. was the Foden agent for decades. It started in the 1930s by selling DG-series Fodens, and this continued after World War II. In 1956 the company was renamed Booth, Poole & Co.. DG-series tippers were operated by the Castle Sand Company based near Dublin.

The Dublin-based Electricity Supply Board (ESB) took delivery of a DG6/70 heavy haulage ballast tractor in May 1947 and this Gardner 6LW-powered 6×4

Above right: Gyptex Ltd, based in Dublin, operated this DG6/15 rigid eight-wheeler, which was powered by a Gardner 6LW engine, producing 102bhp. It also features shiny front wheel covers incorporating the Foden logo. Fleet number 3 was built in 1947 and fitted with a post-war S10 cab. Gyptex produced gypsum wall and ceiling boards. *(Author's collection)*

Right: The Dublin-based Electricity Supply Board (ESB) has always favoured British-built vehicles. It operated several Foden heavy haulage tractors in the past, including this DG6/70, which was delivered in May 1947. It was photographed by a Foden photographer before delivery; the ballast box was built on afterwards. It pulled an old type of drawbar trailer fitted with solid tyres and its job was transporting heavy transformers all over Ireland. ZH1278 still survives and was donated to the transport museum of Dublin for restoration in 1980. *(Author's collection)*

capacity. It was equipped with an extending 90ft boom and 20ft fly jib. A heavy duty "Roballo" type double ball bearing turntable provided a 360 degrees movement of the crane. A Gardner 6LX-150 engine powered this revolutionary chassis. It had a low-mounted cab fitted, placed in front of the double steering front axles. The cab accommodated room for the driver and up to three passengers.

Equipment Sales

In 1967 a company called Equipment Sales Ltd was appointed Foden's sales and service representative for Northern Ireland and the Irish Republic. The Scallon family, which had been in the construction industry for many years, had established the company. It operated Fodens as early as 1947 but realised that slow delivery dates and the poor availability of spare parts put off many potential operators. Although these problems were still present in the late 1960s, Equipment Sales improved this considerably in the early 1970s.

The company built new workshops in Jobstown, in the western part of Dublin, which opened in 1971. It also operated a depot in Omagh, Northern Ireland. Apart from S39 tractor units and rigids, quite a few 4×2 and 6×4 dump trucks were sold to Irish operators in the 1970s. Companies including Dublin-based Roadstone Ltd and John A. Wood Ltd, based in Cork, operated them.

As annual sales of Fodens in the Irish Republic were quite low, Equipment Sales ceased trading from Dublin towards the end of the 1970s. It stayed as Foden agents for Northern Ireland for a while, working from its base in Omagh.

New Dublin Agent

It took until 1986 before Foden appointed a new agent in the Irish Republic. Frank Boland Ltd, based at Naas

tractor was operated until 1974. It was rated to a load capacity of 70 tons, but when the half shafts were replaced by ones having a different ratio the vehicle could take much heavier loads, although only at a reduced speed. ZH1278 was offered to the transport museum of Dublin in 1980, which restored it in its original red ESB livery over a period of six years.

ESB purchased another Foden in 1952, which was a S18-cabbed FGHT8/80 double drive, heavy haulage tractor unit. A Gardner 8LW-150 engine powered the S18-cabbed ballast tractor. It was replaced by a 100-tonne Foden AC33/100 powered by a Cummins

NTK335 engine in the mid-1970s. This machine, 497WZE, is also part of the Dublin transport museum collection. The 6×4 Foden tractor unit was eventually replaced in 1995 by a four-axle ERF EC-series powered by a Cummins N500E engine.

First Crane Carrier

One of the first "Low Line" crane carriers was delivered in 1963 to an Irish operator, the Dublin Erection Company. The four-axle 8×4 driven crane carrier was fitted with a Smith T30 crane, which had a 30 tons lifting

Left: This former British Army drop side truck was built in around 1975. It was sold off by the army in 1979 and re-registered for civilian use. It was subsequently converted into a water tanker and later purchased by the Longford County Fire Service in 1998. It was operated until 2006 and eventually donated to the Longford Vintage Club. *(Colin Stone)*

Right: A mighty S106T4.3406E-455 double drive tractor unit, operated by McMahon Transport & Warehousing from Dublin. It is a 1999 model fitted with the S10 Mk5 Hi-Line cab featuring the Alpha-type grille panel. It was powered by a big Caterpillar 3406E engine, producing 455bhp, which was coupled to an Eaton sixteen-speed gearbox. *(Colin Stone)*

EXPORTS EUROPE

Right: Second generation Foden Alpha vehicles entered service with Irish operators in low numbers. This brand new A3.8RM.C12-400 concrete mixer delivered its load to a housing project at the seaside in Killybegs, County Donegal, in July 2003. The Caterpillar C12-400-powered vehicle was fitted with a Hymix concrete mixer. The Foden was operated by Glenstone, which also operated a lot of Japanese Hino eight-wheelers. *(Wobbe Reitsma)*

Opposite: Another Irish logger, but this time an impressive drawbar combination, crossing a ford at the edge of a forest. It is operated by a County Sligo transport company. The truck was built in 2004 and is powered by a Caterpillar C12-450 engine. The drawbar trailer is an Irish-built Robinson product. *(Colin Stone)*

Right: A hard-working logger in a railway yard at Sligo in the western part of Ireland. It is a A3.6M.ISM420E-XL model dating from 2004, powered by a Cummins ISM420E engine and fitted with the roomy and comfortable XL high roof cab. After intensive use in Ireland this vehicle was exported to Africa, where it is probably still working hard now. *(Colin Stone)*

Above: This early 1960s S21-cabbed FG6/24 tipper was still going strong and earning its keep in April 1993, already more than thirty years old. It was operated by Blokrete, which manufactured building blocks from its plant at Lija near Mosta. It had a Gardner 6LX-150 engine and a locally built tipper body. *(Ian Moxon)*

Above: One of the last Alpha Mark 2 Fodens to be delivered to the Irish Republic was this 2005 model A3.6RT.ISM385E, owned by Beechfield Products. This company has been managed by the Hastings family for more than forty years and operates from Roscrea in County Tipperary. It can provide low-loader, tipper and waste disposal skip services. The Foden is powered by a Cummins ISM385E engine. *(Colin Stone)*

Road in Dublin, became service and parts agent. Foden Ireland, also based in Dublin, was a Foden service agent.

Various 4000 series Fodens were operated in Ireland during the 1980s and 1990s, most of which were imported via Foden dealers in England, Scotland or Northern Ireland. Some Irish operators favoured the new Alpha series, in particular specialist vehicles such as double drive tractors for timber haulage and concrete mixers. Even today there are still some Fodens around in the Irish Republic!

Malta

Working Vintage Vehicles

Malta has been renowned for its ancient buses for many decades. The number of these old and colourful vehicles, which in many cases are operated by owner-drivers, always amaze tourists who visit the islands. However,

Right: Fodens were extremely popular with the Maltese construction companies as they were rugged and strong vehicles even after ten or more years of operation in the UK. Here is a 1974 MG18/24 concrete mixer, powered by a Gardner 6LXB-180 engine, which is operated by Dally Bros Concrete Services. It had a S39 fibreglass non-tilting cab fitted. *(Author's collection)*

Right: This battered FC17 dump truck was still working in 2003 when it was approximately thirty years old. It looks a bit sorry for itself, having no driver's door left and missing a part of its front bumper. Ramal Uzrar operated this dump truck in a Maltese quarry, while he had another one in the yard to break up for spares. *(Peter Seaword)*

Right: Sammut Bros operated this nicely painted S83–cabbed tractor unit, which dates from 1976. The Cummins NHC250-powered unit pulls a two-axle flatbed semi-trailer. Perhaps the Foden meant freedom for the operator (or driver) because that is what he painted in bold lettering on the grille panel. *(Author's collection)*

Below: An RG18/30 model parked up close to the edge of the steep harbour quay. The vehicle was operated by Joseph Caruana Co Ltd, which was based on the island of Gozo. The 30-ton gross weight flatbed truck is loaded with a 20ft sea container and powered by a Gardner 6LXB-180 engine. It dates from around 1977. *(Author's collection)*

Above: Abela Bros is a keen operator of elderly Fodens and this impressive former heavy haulage tractor unit is no exception. It is a double drive AC29/75 model dating from around 1976, which is fitted with a S81 cab and powered by a Cummins NTCE290. This tractor unit was built for heavy haulage applications and was capable of grossing at 75 tons. It is painted in a typical Maltese livery, which is quite attractive. It is pulling an Italian-built OMEP trailer fitted with four separate cement silos. *(Author's collection)*

Left: This is definitely a Foden, which had been operated previously by the British Army for about two decades. The heavy duty front bumper, headlamp set up and the steel S90 cab reveals its former military identity. It most likely is a 58K030R2209 general cargo model, which has right-hand drive. The circa 1978-built truck was powered by a Rolls–Royce Eagle 220 Mark 3 engine and was seen delivering concrete floor parts for a housing scheme in Malta in the late 1990s. *(Pat Crang)*

Right: After a long life with the British Army this 6×4 tanker found a new home in Malta in 2006. The 46P024R2209 model dates from around 1977 and was powered by a Rolls–Royce 220. It delivered fuel to ships at various ports on the island.
(Author's collection)

Right: A Foden MG18/24 concrete mixer is parked up with a Leyland Mastiff and a younger Foden Haulmaster. The mixer chassis dates from 1978 and was fitted with a S80 cab and Gardner 6LXB-180 engine. It was purchased new, operated by Concrete Mix based at Mosta and photographed in April 1993. Concrete Mix ceased trading in the mid-1990s and was renowned for operating many Fodens. *(Ian Moxon)*

Right: The Foden Super Haulmaster range was a special export series that usually went to the Middle East. This 1978 RC29/38 model, fitted with a Cummins NTCE290 engine and a steel S90 cab with left-hand drive, ended up in Malta as a concrete mixer, also working for Concrete Mix of Mosta. *(Ian Moxon)*

Opposite: Carmel Vella Ltd is a building materials supplier based in Naxxar. It operated quite a few British truck makes, including Leyland, AEC, Bedford, Dodge and ERF, and, of course, some Fodens, such as this RG20/30 Haulmaster fitted with a S10 Mark 1 cab and powered by a Gardner 6LXC-201 engine. It was equipped with a heavy duty steel tipper body. *(Author's collection)*

Below: Golden Harvest Flour operated this early 1980s RG20/30 Haulmaster bulk tanker. It shows the S10 Mark 2 composite cab and was powered by a Gardner 6LXC engine, producing 201bhp. It still carried its Foden kite on the grille panel, but has obviously lost its Foden logo. *(Pat Crang)*

Left: Shell UK operated many S106T tractor units fitted with super single tyres on their rear bogies fitted. This tipper is obviously a converted Shell tractor unit operated by the Hidra excavation, demolition and rock cutting company. Before that it was operated by the Maltese transport operator Emmanuel Vella & Sons in 6×4 tractor unit configuration. This immaculate vehicle was powered by a Cummins LT10-250 engine and dates from 1985. *(Pat Crang)*

Right: This 1997 model S106T4-4455, fitted with a high roof XL cab, is now operated by Bonnici Brothers Ltd, moving heavy construction plant, including this Caterpillar 345C hydraulic excavator. Maltese operators are usually proud to indicate what power their vehicles can develop. In this case it is powered by a Caterpillar 3406E engine, producing 455bhp, which is adequate for the job. *(Author's collection)*

cheaper for their operators to buy second-hand vehicles in Britain. However, some companies have bought new, such as the Concrete Mix Limited of Mosta, which bought four new Gardner-powered MG18/24 model concrete mixer chassis fitted with S80 cabs, which entered service towards the end of 1978. These vehicles had British-built, 6 cu m capacity, Ritemixer concrete mixers fitted.

Denmark

Coach

Foden only sold a few vehicles to this small and flat Scandinavian country. The first vehicle was a right-hand drive PVRF6 coach chassis, which was exported to the Copenhagen-based importer F.V. Hein in 1954. It was powered by a six-cylinder Foden FD6 two-stroke engine producing 126bhp, which was fitted transverse at the rear of the chassis. Although the chassis was demonstrated to various operators, it remained unsold two years later. It was then decided to convert it to left-hand drive specification, while a Gardner 6LW replaced the Foden engine. Eventually it was sold to Mr Salomon, a Danish coach operator from Elsinore (Hamlet's home town), who already had several Guy coaches in his fleet. The Foden had a Holger Carlson body fitted, which was transferred to a Volvo coach in 1962 after the Foden was scrapped.

Crane Carriers and Concrete Mixer

It took more than ten years before another Foden chassis entered service in Denmark. This was one of the few Low Line crane carrier chassis to be sold in this country.

one can also see many old commercial vehicles by taking a look in the dock and industrial areas, or just by observing moving vehicles on the public roads. As the Maltese drive on the left-hand side of the road it is very convenient to buy British trucks and many old British trucks received another lease of life there. Even today quite a lot of Fodens are still being operated in the country and most of them were at least ten years old before they hit the roads there. In the late 1990s a lot of different type of Fodens were working very hard for their owners. S21-, S39-, S41-, S80-, S83- and S90-cabbed types could be seen regularly. Younger types such as the S10 mark 1, 2 and 3, and even a single 4000 series, arrived at the turn of the century. Around 2010 the first Foden Alphas appeared on the island. As in Britain, many of these sturdy vehicles work in the construction industry as tippers, concrete mixers or brick carriers.

New Vehicles

It is striking that not many new Fodens were imported by the Maltese. This is probably due to the fact that the vehicles do not do very high mileages, so it is much

Opposite: Crane Hirer BMS from Randers operated this 1965 Low Line crane carrier fitted with a German-built 27-tonne DEMAG K406T crane. It was photographed during a Danish construction equipment exhibition. The DEMAG K406T crane was superseded by the 40-tonne TC120 the following year. This new crane could be fitted by DEMAG on a Foden or Faun crane carrier chassis. *(Richard Blokker collection)*

Right: Faerdigbeton A/S was a Danish operator that took delivery of a Foden vehicle in 1972. The Danish Foden agent Lauritzen was based in Copenhagen. The vehicle was fitted with a 6.5 cu m Ritemixer concrete mixer. The big S41 steel day cab featured a grille panel extension to accommodate the Cummins NH220 engine. *(John Sanderson collection)*

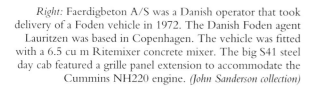

It was fitted with a German DEMAG crane and operated by BMS Crane Hire Company from Randers.

In 1972 an 8×4 concrete mixer chassis fitted with an S41 day cab was delivered to the Faerdigbeton concrete company. The 8C6/26 model Foden was the first four-axle rigid operated in Denmark after Danish legislation permitted such vehicles. The vehicle was powered by a Cummins NHK220 engine and fitted with a 6.5 cu m Ritemixer concrete mixer. It was legally allowed to gross at 26.15 tonnes. Unfortunately, the S41 Foden was only operated for four to five months as its performance at building sites was below the standards set by its operator. It is unknown where it went, but it probably returned to the UK.

Norway

Foden's Norwegian distributor, Maskin A/SK Lund & Co., which was based in Oslo, exhibited Foden dump trucks during various Tekneske Messen (technical exhibitions) in Oslo. It sold some dump trucks into Norway in the 1950s.

Yugoslavia

Dump Trucks

In 1955 a construction company called Konstruktor, based in Split at the Dalmatian coast, took delivery of ten Foden dump trucks. Eight years later it ordered another eight 4×2 FGD6/16 model dump trucks, which were powered by Gardner 6LW engines coupled to Foden twelve-speed gearboxes.

A FGHT8/80 double drive, heavy haulage tractor unit fitted with S18 cab, ballast box and heavy winch was delivered to a Yugoslavian company in 1957.

In 1973, employees of the Yugoslavian Konstruktor company visited Sandbach to be trained for maintaining another ten Leyland-powered, two-axle 4DL6/24 (FL17) dump trucks, which were delivered to this company a little later. The dumpers would initially be operated at tunnelling works and at hydroelectric schemes in Yugoslavia.

Right: One of ten FL17 dump trucks that were delivered in May 1974 to the Yugoslavian company Konstruktor. The Leyland-powered dump truck is leaving one of the tunnels under construction while fully loaded. *(John Sanderson collection)*

Heavy S41 Models

Beograd-based Foden representatives also sold small numbers of 8×4 tipper chassis, which were fitted with S41 steel cabs. Some of these vehicles had very powerful turbocharged Cummins NTC335 engines, similar to the ones exported to Greece.

More left-hand drive models were exported to Yugoslavia in the mid-1970s in 6×4 tractor unit form, which could gross at 60 tonnes. Some of the S41-cabbed vehicles had steel double roofs fitted, which also acted as sun visors.

Italy

Several dump trucks were exported to Italy in the 1950s and 1960s. They worked in quarries and at steel works, moving scrap and furnace waste. Foden dump trucks were exhibited regularly during the Milan Fairs in the 1950s to advertise the product.

Rome-based Fiorentini crane manufacturers used Foden crane carriers as a mobile base for its products in the 1960s.

Austria

Very few Fodens were operated in this small Alpine country. At least one ancient three-axle DG6/10 chassis was operated there in the late 1940s and early 1950s. It was fitted with drop sides covered with tarpaulins and pulled a matching two-axle drawbar trailer.

An Austrian contractor, based in Vienna, took delivery of a 6×4 twin-cab crane carrier fitted with a

Right: Some powerful RC33/34 models were exported to Yugoslavia in 1974. They had Cummins NTC335 engines and left-hand drive S41 steel cabs. This vehicle shows the huge steel tipper body in raised position. Bosnaputevi operated it in and around Sarajevo, which is now the capital of the Republic of Bosnia–Herzegovina. *(Fodens Ltd)*

Opposite: An old DG6/10 is having a rest at the roadside in Austria. The vehicle was operated by Weismann Transport and probably dates from 1942. Both truck and drawbar trailer have drop side bodies, covered with tarpaulins. It is probably the only Foden ever operated in Austria. *(Author's collection)*

Below: This 1966 left-hand drive Low Line crane carrier chassis is on its way to Wilhelm Hagenkamp KG based in Langenfeld (Germany). The model CC8/12.30 chassis/cab would be fitted with a 30-tonne Wilhag AK3010 crane, constructed by Hagenkamp. The chassis was shipped to Rotterdam and then driven to Germany, passing Holland, hence its warning sign fitted to the front of the cab, which says in Dutch 'Dangerous – Wide Vehicle'. *(Richard Blokker collection)*

Jones KL15-25 crane in 1963. It made the trip under its own power, taking the Felixstowe–Rotterdam ferry and made the overland trip via the German motorways to arrive in the set time.

Germany

Due to import restrictions, Foden was not able to sell vehicles to Germany during the late 1940s and 1950s. Still, there was one wartime DG-series 6×4 Foden used by a German operator. The steel merchant that operated it had converted the S10 cab into a narrow one-man cab. As the cab was placed in the middle of the chassis it could transport long protruding steel girders at both sides of the body.

The German DEMAG crane manufacturer took delivery of many Foden FC and Low Line crane carrier chassis in the 1950s and 1960s. DEMAG used the chassis as a base for its wide range of cranes and excavators. Foden even adapted the crane carrier chassis to fit German-built air-cooled Deutz engines. Most vehicles were delivered overland to DEMAG's factory in Dusseldorf.

Russia

Not many Foden vehicles were sold to Russia but Autoexport of Moscow, a state-owned import and export company, ordered a couple of heavy duty S21-cabbed 8×4 tippers in 1964. It is not known where the tippers were operated but they looked very impressive with their double-skin cab roofs and heavy tipping bodies.

A major order was obtained from the British government in 1993. It ordered twenty-five heavy S108T4-4465 model 8×4 tractor units, which were destined for the Russian Army. The vehicles were used for the transport of dismantled nuclear weapons. They were powered by Cummins NTAA465 engines and had to operate in areas where temperatures dropped to -40 degrees C.

Finally, quite a few second-hand Fodens were imported into the country in the first decade of the 21st century. So, don't be too surprised if you see 3000-series concrete mixers running in the streets of Moscow.

Above: The Russian state-owned Autoexport company did not only export Russian cars and trucks, but it also imported commercial vehicles. This impressive FG6/24 tipper is one of two vehicles that were exported to the USSR in 1964. They had Gardner 6LX-150 engines and were fitted with special S21 export cab, which featured a double roof that also acted as a sun shield for driver and mate. *(Author's collection)*

CHAPTER TWO

Exports Americas

It is striking that Foden never had a representative in the United States of America. but most other European truck manufacturers did not attempt to enter this market either, because it differed so much from the European market. The Americans favoured bonneted trucks provided with lots of horsepower and large custom-built sleeper cabs. Legislation on lengths and weights was also completely different. It was not until the last quarter of the 20th century that Volvo became successful in the USA by taking over White, and eventually selling Volvo-powered trucks all over the country. The only Fodens that could be seen in the USA were some models that were tested by Paccar after the takeover in 1980 and a number of Kenworth-badged 4000 series 6×4 oil-well trucks, which were operated worldwide by the Schlumberger organisation.

Canada

Five or six Foden steamers were exported to Canada between 1910 and 1915. Most were 5-ton Colonial steamers, which were specially designed for export. The first Foden steamer was purchased by John Duncan in 1910, soon followed by a second one. The City of New Westminster in British Columbia purchased two 5-ton Colonial steam wagons in 1913.

Two war-type DG6/10 Fodens were operated for many years by a Canadian company called J.R. Sercombe & Son, which was based in Toronto. They had been converted into 6×4 tractor units, pulling low-loaders with machinery or heavy plant that weighed up to 40 tonnes! Foden's general sales manager, George Dean, visited Canada in 1948 to assess the possibilities to sell Fodens into Canada. Unfortunately this did not materialise, but they did export some dump trucks in the 1950s and 1960s.

Schlumberger also operated Foden Alpha-type oil survey vehicles in Canada in 6×4 configuration at the beginning of the 21st century.

Above: A 1959 left-hand drive FED4/18 dump truck that was operated in the Niagara Falls area by Steve McKee. The 18-ton gross weight vehicle was not fitted with the standard half cab but with a more roomy and comfortable S20 export cab with a double skin roof. *(Julian Hollinshead collection)*

Left: A 5-ton Colonial steamer that was supplied to the city of New Westminster in British Columbia in 1913. The drop side tipper body is fitted with an early type of spreader equipment. It was one of two steamers that were operated by the city council. *(David Bloor collection)*

Jamaica

Foden was represented in Jamaica from 1954 by Kingston Industrial Agencies Ltd. This Foden sales and service organisation was based at the outskirts of Kingston. The company was very active in selling quite a few Fodens on the island. During the 1950s FG-type vehicles fitted with S18 cabs were put into service by local operators. They included FGTU6/25 heavy tractor units for the transportation of earth moving equipment. Towards the end of the 1950s the first S20-cabbed vehicles, fitted with insulated double roofs, arrived in Jamaica. They included 4×2 and heavy duty 6×4 tractor units, but also three-axle FG6/20 concrete mixers. The Jamaican agents were quite successful during this period and sold ten to fifteen vehicles a year, which was quite an achievement in such a small market. Foden dump trucks played a major role in a large housing scheme in the 1960s, when nearly 10,000 houses were built at Kingston's Harbour View.

Nowadays one can still find some Foden trucks in Jamaica, as the Jamaican Truckers Linkup on Facebook revealed! Although the majority of the trucks on the island are built in the USA, there is still the odd Foden Alpha running up and down.

Opposite: This elegant tractor–trailer unit was built in 1966 for B. Elliott, a machine tool producer from London. The Crane–Fruehauf semi-trailer acted as a mobile showroom for its products. It was built by Norwich Coachworks for service in North and South America. Norwich Coachworks also built the large crew cab, featuring rectangular French Cibie lights that were also fitted to the S24-cabbed models. The model 4AC6/30 could gross at 30 tons and was powered by a Cummins NHE195, which could be serviced by most truck dealers in America. The 42ft combination had a top speed of 56mph. The trailer was equipped with air conditioning, detachable roof panels to load large machines and a 15KVA generator/transformer, which could convert outside-sourced currents into 400 volts or could be used independently. *(Author's collection)*

Above: Most Fodens exported to Jamaica were S18 and S20 models that entered the Caribbean island in the 1950s and 1960s. However, some Gardner 6LXB-180 front-engined bus chassis were delivered in 1976. The BG18/16 models were bodied by Belgian body builders Jonckheere and featured folding front and rear doors. Passengers had to board at the rear door and leave the vehicle at the front. *(Peter Tulloch collection)*

Argentina

Long before World War II Foden already had an agent in this country to sell Foden steam engines and steam wagons, which were quite popular there in the 1920s and 1930s. Banham Bros was the agent and it sold more steam lorries before World War II than diesel-powered vehicles after it. Despite severe import restrictions, ten DG type four-, six- and eight-wheel lorries found their way to Argentina shortly after the hostilities ceased. The shipment from Liverpool of another ten Fodens, which were on their way there in 1947, was frustrated by these restrictions. These vehicles eventually ended up in Australia and South Africa.

Some DG-series eight-wheelers eventually did arrive in Argentina. They pulled drawbar trailers, which were allowed to carry payloads of 36 tons – 50 per cent more than the maximum gross combination weights of vehicles in Britain at the time. Most of these vehicles, which were exported to Argentina around 1946–47, were still going strong in the early 1960s. In 1947 one PVSC6 bus chassis, powered by a Gardner 6LW engine, was sent to Argentina and sold to an unknown operator.

Opposite: A substantial export order was shipped to Argentina in 1947. Seven DG4/7.5 four-wheelers, one DG6/12 six-wheeler and two DG6/15 eight-wheelers were craned on to a cargo ship in Glasgow. They were loading using a floating crane, which was mounted on a barge and operated by Sir William Arrol & Co. Ltd of Glasgow. This impressive photograph shows the DG6/12 craned on board and two DG6/15s still on the barge's deck, while the man in the foreground is reading a newspaper! All DG-series trucks were destined for Foden's agents in Argentina, Banham Bros of Buenos Aires, which was stamped on every vehicle's door. *(David Bloor collection)*

Below: Senor Munoz still operated two DG-series eight-wheelers in the early 1960s. They did 1,800km round trips between Bahia Blanca, Mar del Plata and the Argentine capital city of Buenos Aires. The DG series were built in 1947 and 1948 and pulled two-axle drawbar trailers. They carried foodstuffs at average payloads of 36 tons! *(Foden News, May 1960)*

Right: Foden steam lorries, in Spanish "Camions a Vapor", were extremely popular in Argentina. These two steamers were exhibited during a commercial vehicle show in Buenos Aires in 1930. The Speed Six (or O type) model was a two-axle rigid, which could carry a payload of 6 tons, while the heavier three-axle Speed Twelve (or Q type) model could handle 10 tons. These vehicles could easily achieve top speeds of around 60mph, but were limited by Foden to 45mph. Needless to say, quite a few operators adjusted their vehicles to increase their top speeds. *(John Sanderson collection)*

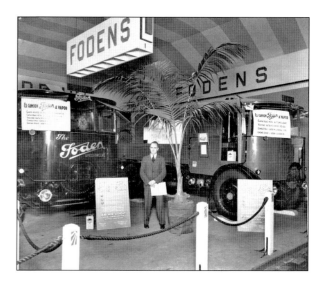

Brazil

According to a Foden steam wagon brochure, some 5-ton Colonial steamers were supplied to the Brazilian government around 1915.

Shortly after World War II a number of Foden DG-type lorries were exported to Brazil and sold to customers in Rio de Janeiro and Porto Alegre. Two rear-engined PVRG6 buses, powered by Gardner 6LW engines, were delivered in 1951. They were operated by the Olavi Ika company, which was based in Rio de Janeiro.

FG-series vehicles were imported in small quantities in the 1950s. Some of these vehicles worked as timber tractor units, which were coupled to single-axle pole trailers. They took out timber from Brazilian forests; it was not uncommon for the trailers to be loaded with huge tree trunks, which weighed a staggering 25 tonnes.

Right: Some Foden tractor units fitted with S18 cabs went to Brazil, where they worked as logging tractors, pulling pole trailers. This testimony of a Brazilian operator says enough about the harsh conditions they had to work in. They could easily take 25,000kg of timber, which was about 24 (British) tons and 12 cwt. It is obvious that the operator, Agro Madeireira Peres Ltda, was quite pleased with his Foden. *(Foden News, January 1956)*

FROM BRAZIL
—but no translation is necessary!
except, perhaps, 25,000 quilos equals 24 tons, 12 cwts.

AgroMadeireira Peres Ltda.
SERRARIA PERES
MADEIRAS — CEREAIS — CAFÉ — PECUÁRIA
São Pedro dos Ferros — E. F. Leopoldina — Minas Gerais — End. Teleg. AMPÉRES

São Pedro dos Ferros, 19th august 1955

Fodens Ltda.
Elworth Works
Sandbach - Cheshire
England

Gentlemen:

We are herewith enclosing a picture of one of your trucks, which is employed by us in our forests to take out timber.
This particular truck is loaded with three logs totaling 25.000 quilos(twenty five thousend quilos). We use in our operations several types of gas and Diesel trucks. However, your truck has proved over thousands of miles of forests roads to be most reliable and we can say— THE BEST!

Yours very truly
by Agro Madeireira Peres Ltda.,

CHAPTER THREE

Exports Africa

South Africa

Steamers Rule

Nearly every type of Foden steamer was exported to South Africa in the first part of the 20th century. This country was an important export market for steamers for a very long time. The first Foden steamer entered South Africa in 1902 and was put into service by George Harris of Bramfontein (Transvaal). Early traction engines, 3-, 4- and 5-ton wagons, and C and D types were shipped to South Africa and even some Foden Agritractors and Speed Six and Twelve models found their way to customers in the most southern part of this big continent. In 1934 the Fowler Tar Spraying Company imported the last two overtype steam wagons built by Foden.

Things changed in the 1930s when petrol and early diesel-powered lorries became more popular in Europe. South Africa was not far behind as Foden exhibited its new range of "Diesel" vehicles during the Empire Exhibition in Johannesburg, which was held from September 1936 until January 1937. Guest, Sykes Ltd, which represented Fodens in South Africa from 1936 onwards, was highly involved in an extensive sales campaign to bring the new diesel models into the South African limelight. The famous Foden Motor Works Band was engaged to play at the exhibition for five to six weeks. It resulted in the export of quite a few four and six-wheeled trucks and tractor units fitted with the DG-type S9 cab, which showed an exposed radiator. Companies including the Fowler Tar Spraying Co., Springs Crushers, Bagley & Steventon, Jackson Transport and ABC Transport operated them.

African Branch

Saker Bartle (South Africa) Ltd, which had workshops in Johannesburg, Durban, Port Elizabeth and Cape Town, represented Foden in South Africa in the 1940s. Two years after World War II, about six vehicles a month left Elworth Works in Sandbach to be shipped to Bartle's. It took until 1948 before Foden introduced new models. Up to that year most vehicles were still derivatives of the ubiquitous pre-war DG series, which were sold to well-known South African operators such as Thorntons, Lyon's, Primrose Brick Works and Ross' Transport. Regular visits from Foden directors and engineers contributed to the production of purpose-built vehicles to meet South African specifications as much as possible.

Right: The late Sam Satterthwaite, who passed away in 1996 at the age of nearly 87, poses in front of a 1931 Speed Six steam lorry pulling two drawbar trailers. The Speed Six was Foden's first pneumatic-tyred steam wagon to enter South Africa. Sam was doing demonstrations for Foden in South Africa during the early 1930s. (*John Sanderson collection*)

As Foden saw very good opportunities for selling its new S18 models in South Africa, it set up its own branch at Eloff Street Extension in Johannesburg in 1950. Mr E. Twemlow, one of Foden's directors, was sent to the republic to make the necessary arrangements. Harold Hymans, a Scottish engineer who was working for Bartle's, was appointed managing director. He kept this position for fifteen years until he died during a visit to Britain aged 67. New premises were opened in 1951 and Fodens (SA) Pty Ltd sold many S18 and dump truck models to South African operators during the 1950s. Early crane carrier chassis, some coaches and small FE models were also sold in the same decade. Due to increasing sales, Fodens SA expanded by enlarging its premises in Eloff Street Extension in 1954.

Developing 1950s

S18-cabbed models were exported to South Africa in all available axle configurations, from simple 4×2 trucks to heavy duty 8×4 tractor units. Lightweight OG4/6 tractor units and rigid models were also shipped to the country, but in smaller numbers. Most vehicles were shipped from Liverpool in chassis form, many times as deck cargo. Tyres, cabs and dump truck bodies were fitted after the chassis arrived in South Africa. The S18 and OG cabs were locally built and looked slightly different in comparison with the British factory-built cabs. Well-known companies such as Metal Box, Hume Pipe Co., Thorntons, Nigel Bottling Co., B&B Removals, OK Bazaars and others operated many S18-cabbed Fodens during and, in some cases long after, the 1950s.

Quite a few heavy haulage tractors in 6×4 and 8×4 configuration were sold to leading civil and public companies. The well-known Thorntons Transportation Ltd of Johannesburg operated a number of FGHT8/80 four-axle heavy haulage tractor units during the 1950s. They were powered by the big Gardner 8LW-150 engine, which was fitted with a massive radiator protruding the S18 cab. Thorntons also operated smaller S18-cabbed 6×4 tractor units. Five 6×4 tractor units fitted with S18 cabs and heavy winches were delivered to the Provincial Administration in Transvaal in 1950.

One of the most striking S18-cabbed rigid eights was a mobile weighbridge tester that was delivered to the South African Department of Commerce and Industries in 1957. The well-known British Foden agent Sam Satterthwaite, who ran Streetly Garage in Streetly near Birmingham, developed the vehicle's van body and equipment. The whole outfit weighed a staggering 27 tons, including 15 tons of weights, which were stored in the van body. These could be lowered on to weighbridges by a gantry crane fitted horizontally to the roof of the body. The mobile weighbridge tester had to test the 700–800 weighbridges in South Africa annually, which took about eight months to cover.

The lightweight Foden FE4/8 two-stroke models were also popular in South Africa. They were operated in the distribution industry for delivering Coca-Cola soft drinks, bottled by the Nigel Bottling Co., or delivering building materials to small contractors. Greyhound Bus Service took delivery of a handsome long distance coach chassis. Quite a few crane carrier chassis and complete dump trucks also found their way to the country in the 1950s. The Pretoria Portland Cement Company was one of the many South African companies that operated Foden dump trucks in the mid-1950s. Most of the ten-strong fleet had S18 type cabs fitted.

Left: Thorntons FGHT8/80 four-axle tractor unit, built in 1952, is seen here transporting an 80-ton winding engine drum to the Randfontein Gold Mine in Transvaal province. The massive 24 × 14ft drum sat on the bed of a heavy girder trailer. The tractor unit was powered by the big eight-in-line Gardner 8LW-150 engine. *(Author's collection)*

Right: Sam Satterthwaite, who ran Streetley Garage near Birmingham, designed and built the bodywork of this mobile weighbridge tester. Fodens SA Pty Ltd delivered it in 1957 to the South African Department of Commerce & Industries. It was fitted with an S18 crew cab and a van body, which accommodated the 15 tons of weights that were needed for testing weighbridges all over the country. A Gardner 6LW-112 engine coupled to a Foden 12-speed gearbox powered the FG6/24 model. *(Henk Veldkamp)*

Booming 1960s

Foden lorries aroused an ever-growing demand in the republic during the 1960s. As a result, Foden could not supply enough vehicles to the South African market. It was decided in 1965 that Foden's premises and plant would be increased considerably. Vehicles were sent to South Africa in kit form and assembled locally at the Johannesburg depot. It gave Fodens SA the opportunity to tailor the chassis and cabs to its customers' requirements. The Johannesburg depot had assembly, construction and repair sections. There were Foden agents in Durban, Port Elizabeth and Cape Town to support customers in all parts of the republic.

The new S20 cabs had a certain amount of locally manufactured parts and as a result they looked a little different in comparison with their British counterparts. Although the S20 shape was still clearly recognisable, visible differences were the doors, front wings, windscreens, and on later models the slightly protruding grille panels. They were built throughout the 1960s as the fibreglass S21 fixed cab and S24 tilt cabs were not available in South Africa.

By expanding its facilities, Fodens SA was able to cut down delivery times and satisfy customer demand. Loyal customers such as Nigel Bottling took delivery of several S20-cabbed Fodens, including twin-steer chassis fitted with drop side bodies. Its fleet of Foden vehicles made it possible to deliver up to 400,000 cases of Coca-Cola drinks annually. Several pulled four-wheel drawbar trailers to increase their payload. Norman's Transport Lines was another customer, which operated many S20 tractor units and rigids to fulfil its contract with Consolidated Glassworks (Consol). More than 4,000 tons of glass bottles and other glassware were transported every month. South African Breweries used S20-cabbed tractor units to distribute its Castle beer to the furthest corners of the country. The O.K. Bazaars was another customer that operated S20 type tractor units. The Johannesburg-based company used eleven Fodens in the early 1960s to supply its big stores based all over the republic. S20-cabbed heavy haulage units in 6×4 configuration could be seen regularly in South Africa; Thorntons even operated four-axle units.

A Foden product that became very popular in South Africa was the dump truck range. This was not only with private companies but also with the Department of Water Affairs, which used many of them for the construction of major water works, such as irrigation canals and dams. The locally assembled dump trucks, which were manufactured from the mid-1960s, also featured different looking half cabs. Again, the South African half cab had the same shape as the Sandbach-built vehicle, but the door, roof and side windows were a little different. The most striking differences were the front wings, which had sloping edges instead of the normal curved versions. Finally, locally assembled dump trucks had no additional window below the front windscreen.

Above: Norman's Transport Lines Ltd had an exclusive contract to transport the products manufactured by Consolidated Glassworks Ltd (brand name Consol) throughout the South African republic. For that purpose it put into service six new FGTU6/25 tractor units in 1962, which were powered by Gardner 6LX-150 engines. (*John Sanderson collection*)

Opposite: South African S20 Fodens had locally built cabs, which looked a bit different in comparison with their British counterparts. Although looking like S20 cabs at first sight, windscreens, grille panels and doors were shaped differently. Fleet number 18 was one of several Foden S20s operated by Saunders of Edenvale. The vehicles carried explosives in their low height van bodies. The S20 was photographed in the yard of Explo Carriers (James Sydney) in July 1982. The FG6/20 model vehicle dates from October 1966. (*Henk Veldkamp*)

Left: Also fitted with the locally built S20 cab is this heavy 6×4 tractor unit operated by Longhauls Pty Ltd from Pietermaritzburg. It is obvious that fleet number 17 needed a bit of maintenance as the fitter's tools can be seen next to the rear wheels. *(John Sanderson collection)*

Right: Thorntons was a renowned Foden user that operated quite a few heavy haulage tractor units in the 1950s and 1960s. This four-axle FCHT6/80 tractor unit, fitted with a locally built S20 type cab, moves a fractionate tower for the oil industry weighing 70 tons. The tractor unit has a manually operated double hub-reduction system and pulls a three-axle low-loader trailer. An additional carrier, featuring three axle rows of eight wheels, supports the back end of the tower. The Cummins NH220-powered outfit, dating from around 1960, was photographed in April 1968. *(Author's collection)*

Right: The Nigel Bottling Co. was South Africa's authorised Coca-Cola bottler from 1949. It was a major Foden user and favoured two-stroke engines. This FE6/14 model dates from 1962 and was powered by a Foden FD6 Mark 6 two-stroke engine, which developed 175bhp. The vehicle's power was adequate to pull a drawbar trailer. The company was based in Nigel, Transvaal. *(David Bloor collection)*

Left: Dump trucks were popular vehicles in South Africa. The cabs were locally assembled and differed from their British counterparts. The most striking difference was their trapezium formed front wings. The British-built versions had curved ones. This six-wheel dump truck was delivered to G.D. Rossouw Mine Transport Corporation in the late 1960s. The company was founded in the early 1950s and removed gold mine waste such as rock and sand from the mine shafts near Johannesburg. *(David Bloor collection)*

Flourishing 1970s

The first Fodens fitted with fibreglass cabs were S36 type vehicles. The first ones arrived in South Africa at the end of the 1960s. Later models had the S39 cab fitted. Most were 4×2 tractor units, of which many had Gardner 6LXB-180 engines. The O.K. Bazaars was one operator that purchased them. Later in the 1970s Cummins engines were favoured, especially in 6×4 heavy haulage tractor unit form. South African Fodens could also be fitted with Rolls–Royce Eagle engines.

In April 1972 Foden opened new premises at Alberton near Johannesburg. The new building offered work for eighty people in the offices and workshops.

The new depot was situated on a 6.5-acre site, while the workshops and offices took some 33,000 sq ft. Foden was already well represented in the South African commercial vehicle market and these new premises made it possible to increase the assembly of Foden vehicles significantly. Initially Fodens SA hoped to produce five vehicles a week, but higher outputs were easy to achieve as there was ample room for future expansion.

During the 1970s Fodens SA sold many vehicles fitted with a locally manufactured steel S60 cab. This cab had a striking appearance by having a forward-sloping windscreen. These vehicles became very popular in 6×4 rigid and tractor specifications, although 4×2 tractor units and 8×4 rigids were also sold. Auto

Carriers Transport took delivery of twenty 4×2 tractor units in 1974. These S60-cabbed units were powered by Cummins NH220 engines and clocked up mileages of up to 150,000 annually, delivering cars to all parts of the country. Fodens SA even built some special

Below: Locally built steel S60 cabs were quite popular with South African operators in the early 1970s. Afrovan operated this nice 4×2 tractor unit fitted with a crew cab in combination with double removal semi-trailers, featuring large side doors, which were manufactured of aluminium. Fleet number 36 made regular round trips of 2,000 miles between Cape Town and Johannesburg throughout the 1970s. *(Author's collection)*

Left: Another nearly identical crew-cabbed tractor unit fitted with the South African steel S60 cab pulling double trailers. Pickfords Road Services operated in South Africa with this 45-ton gross weight 4AC6/45 model, which was powered by a Cummins NHK220 engine. The outfit dates from 1971. *(Julian Hollinshead collection)*

Right: The South African branch of Pioneer Concrete operated this concrete mixer fitted with a locally built S60 cab and powered by a Gardner 6LXB-180 engine. The D73 model was built in 1974 and had a locally built concrete mixer fitted to its chassis. *(Fodens Ltd)*

Below: Fodens SA built some very impressive drilling rigs for Frankipile's South African branch. The five-axle vehicles in 10×4 configuration were built around 1975 and fitted with the locally built steel S60 cab. A heavy bracket, which is fitted to the vehicle's front bumper, supports the drilling boom. This one is photographed in Fodens SA yard in Alberton, near Johannesburg. *(Author's collection)*

Left: Four three-axle rigid trucks were delivered to Longhauls in the mid-1970s. They were fitted with half cabs and specially designed bodies for sugar cane harvesting. They could gross at 22 tons, but by using an additional drawbar trailer this could be raised to a 38-ton gross combination weight. *(David Bloor collection)*

Right: Not many Fodens were used for refuse collection services. Waste-tech, which operated many refuse collection vehicles and landfill sites in South Africa, was sold in 1997 to Enviroserv Waste Management. Fleet number 26 was a 6XB6/24 model dating from 1973 and was powered by the reliable Gardner 6LXB-180 engine. Note the different head lamp arrangement of the S80 cab; British S80 cabs had 11in single headlamps, while the South African models featured smaller double headlamps. *(Author's collection)*

Opposite: This RG18/24 model Foden is fitted with a dual-purpose body, which features glass racks at both sides of the vehicle, a split flatbed with head and tailboards and a loading crane. Fleet number 640 was operated by Express Glass Works and photographed when new in front of Foden's South African premises in 1975. It is also fitted with the locally built S80 cab. *(Fodens Ltd)*

Below: Ready Mix Concrete SA operated this mobile concrete pump, which is fitted on a RG18/30 model eight-wheel chassis. The Gardner 6LXB-180 powered vehicle was built in 1975. It had a locally built version of the British S80 cab, which featured a sleeper or crew cab extension. Initially working for the Cape Town RMC depot, the vehicle was transferred to Transvaal in 1979, when this photograph was taken. *(Henk Veldkamp)*

Left: Ruto Flour Mills from Pretoria operated this impressive AC29/45 model six-wheel tractor unit, which was powered by a 14-litre Cummins NTC290 engine and fitted with the locally built S80 cab. *(Author's collection)*

Right: The fibreglass S83 cab was also available in South Africa, although they were built locally and featured some different cab panels and headlamp arrangement. This 8RR model tanker operated by Sasol was built in 1977. A powerful Rolls–Royce 265L engine made this vehicle a real flyer. *(Author's collection)*

Left: The Alberton Municipality, hometown of Fodens SA, ordered six BG18/16 model single deck buses in 1975. They had locally built Brockhouse bodies fitted and were powered by reliable Gardner 6LXB-180 engines. This new bus range was also sold to some other South African municipalities. *(Author's collection)*

Right: NP50849 was another BG18/16 bus model that entered service with Ghetty's Motor Transport (Pty) Ltd from Pietermaritzburg in the mid-1970s. It is seen here leaving a bus station in heavy rain. It was powered by a front-mounted Gardner 6LXB-180 engine. *(Peter Tulloch collection)*

92

10×4 rigid chassis, which were operated by drilling companies. The heaviest S60-cabbed Fodens were two long wheelbase 8×4 tractor units built for the Department of Water Affairs. They were equipped with 60-ton winches and 7-ton Hiab loading cranes. The vehicles were powered by Cummins NTC400 engines and had Allison CLBT5860 automatic transmissions. The tractor units were designed for 100-ton gross weight operations to move construction equipment. This organisation had a fleet of more than 250 Fodens at the time, being the biggest Foden customer outside the UK.

Alongside the S60-cabbed Fodens, the fibreglass S80 tilt cab became available for the South African market. Besides the 4×2 and 6×4 tractor units, rigid eights became also popular during the 1970s. Most South African S80 type vehicles had double headlights instead of the standard 11in single headlights, which were common in the UK. Most S80/S83 cabs were locally manufactured and marketed as Duracabs.

Alberton Municipality, the hometown of Fodens SA, ordered six BG18/16 single-deck bus chassis in 1975. These front-engined, Gardner 6LXB-powered buses had locally built bodies fitted by Brockhouse Ltd. Neighbouring Germiston municipality ordered another eight chassis, with a possible repeat order for a further four.

Foden dump trucks continued to sell very well in South Africa. The Department of Water Affairs ordered its first Foden dump truck in 1956 and had 155 of

Right: This C221 model dump truck is the equivalent of the British FC27A dump truck. It was one of three which were delivered to Moolman Bros based in Pine Town. The locally built half cab showed some resemblance with the S51 cab, although most cab panels had different shapes. A Cummins NK855 engine, which produced 310bhp, powered these vehicles. They were operated at a railway line construction job in the Healy District. *(Author's collection)*

Opposite: Dump truck chassis fitted with half cabs were also used for concrete mixer applications. This Cummins-powered model was fitted with a South African-built Copelyn truck mixer. Copelyn nowadays produces tipping semi-trailers. *(Author's collection)*

these vehicles in operation in 1975. The dump trucks delivered in the 1970s could be recognised by their forward-sloping windscreens, which were similar to their British S51 counterparts.

Terminal Tractors

Terminal tractors are used on industrial estates and in dock areas, where having a registration plate and type approval is not always necessary. Foden had not produced such vehicles in the past and the initial order for 138 "Dockspotters" by South African Railways (SAR) in 1977 was welcomed with pleasure at a time when Foden's order books were not full. The prototype was built at Foden's factory in Alrode in 1977.

Production chassis were built in Sandbach and shipped to Cape Town in kit form. After arrival in South-Africa, Fodens SA built up the chassis at their

Below: In 1977 and 1978 Fodens SA built 169 Dockspotters for the South African Railways. The chassis were built from kits supplied by Foden UK. They were equipped with elevating fifth wheels, a locally built half cab with rear entry and were powered by Cummins NHC230 engines. They could handle gross weights of up to 50 tonnes. Terminal tractors SAS-V 9652 and 9653 are seen here in a South African harbour ready to start their first jobs. *(Author's collection)*

Alrode premises. The cabs were locally built and featured rear entry. The tractor units were powered by Cummins NTC 230 engines, which were coupled to Allison HT470D four-speed automatic gearboxes. The front axle had a capacity of eight tonnes, while the rear axle could carry 17 tonnes. The vehicles, which were fitted with hydraulically operated, elevating fifth wheels, were designed for gross combination weights of up to 50 tonnes. In total 169 Dockspotters were delivered to SAR in 1977 and 1978.

Locally Built Cabs

In January 1978, managing director David Foden came over to South Africa to announce a new range of Foden

Above: A fine example of the sturdy Foden 8×4 chassis fitted with a locally built cab featuring some British S95 and S10 Mark 1 Fleetmaster/Haulmaster cab parts. The tipper body was also built in South Africa. This vehicle was photographed prior to delivery to the customer in around 1980. *(John Sanderson collection)*

Left: The front cover of this 1978 South African brochure clearly shows that most South African Foden vehicles were fitted with locally built cabs. The RC35/50 rigid eight-wheeler is fitted with such a cab, which also has a sleeper cab extension. Some panels of the steel S90 cab, including the hinged fibreglass grille panel, were used for this product. This tilt cab was introduced in January 1978. The "Duracab" was built from S80 cab components and featured smaller windscreens and smaller double headlamps. The Fleetmaster cab was a standard UK product. The brochure is printed in English and Afrikaans, which is derived from the Dutch language. *(Author's collection)*

vehicles, including the Fleetmaster range fitted with the S90 or S95 steel cab. The second new vehicle was a RC35/50 Haulmaster rigid eight chassis, powered by a Cummins NTC350 engine. The chassis was fitted with a new locally built Santini tilt cab, which had a S90 type grille panel incorporated. Access to the front of the engine was possible by a hinged radiator, which could be tilted forward. The cab was available in day and sleeper cab version. Later versions had a black S10 Fleetmaster type grille panel, smaller Foden kite and double headlamps, which were fitted in black mountings. A high roof, double bunk, version was introduced a little later. The sleeper cab versions had a striking rearward fitted sleeper extension. The cab was equipped with the tilting system and interior of the Foden S95. This model was extremely popular in 6×4 tractor unit form. In standard

Left: Frasers operated this heavy haulage tractor, which is equipped with a locally built high roof sleeper cab. It featured some S10 cab components and pulled a Nicolas modular trailer, which is loaded with a heavy O & K excavator. Fleet number 142, built in the early 1980s, was powered by a Cummins NTE400 engine. Model 6AC40/140 could handle gross weights of up to 140 tons. *(D.A. Child)*

Right: Hultrans had a large transport fleet that included quite a few Fodens. The locally built Foden 6×4 tractor unit was the most popular axle configuration, particularly in heavy haulage tractor form. Fleet number 446 shows red warning flags at both cab front corners and is loaded with a Komatsu dump truck chassis. This model 6AC35/65 has a Cummins NTE350 engine and was probably built in 1980. *(Author's collection)*

Above: Another model 6AC35/65 heavy haulage tractor, this time loaded with a Caterpillar D7A crawler tractor. This short wheelbase, 6×4 tractor unit had a design gross weight of 65 tons. A Cummins NTE350 was the popular engine choice in 1981. *(Author's collection)*

form they had Cummins NTE290 or NTC350 engines, but more powerful Cummins and a range of Rolls–Royce engines could be ordered as an option. Quite a few of these 6×4 tractor unit chassis fitted with the locally built Santini cab were exported to Zimbabwe. An 8×4 tractor unit for heavy haulage applications up to 140 tons gross weight became available from 1979 onwards. South African Railways took delivery of most of them for its heavy haulage division.

The most striking vehicle that was built on a Foden chassis was a four-axle, 8×4 driven, fire engine, which went into service with the Alberton Municipality in early 1980. A Cummins NTA 400 engine powered

the 11m long vehicle; the engine was coupled to an automatic transmission. It could reach a speed of more than 65 miles per hour, carried 15,000 litres of water and also had 4,000 litres of foam on board, which could be spread by a roof-mounted foam cannon with a reach of 60m. The Safire Fomobile body and fire equipment was supplied by Hotline Fire Equipment of Germiston. The whole outfit weighed a staggering 36 tons and could be operated by a two-man crew. The vehicle, with code number B 11, was still operated by the City Council of Alberton nearly twenty-five years later. It was in an immaculate condition and had only done 9,798km by January 2004.

Left: Special Foden cab plates, showing the Foden logo and old style South African flag, were attached to all locally built Foden vehicles during the 1970s and 1980s. *(Author's collection)*

Right: In early 1980, the Alberton Municipality purchased this immaculate Foden fire engine. It was equipped with a Safire Fomobile body, which carried the necessary equipment but also 15,000 litres of water and 4,000 litres of foam. A 400bhp Cummins NTE engine gave ample power for a top speed of more than 100kph. The big foam cannon had a reach of 60m. *(Henk Veldkamp)*

Declining 1980s

Fodens SA won a prestigious blue riband award for the third time in succession in 1981. The award was conducted by South African Transport magazine for the best payload productivity figures achieved by commercial vehicles. A 6RC37/65 three-axle truck and three-axle drawbar trailer won the award in this year after a gruelling test against an ERF. The combination could gross at 65 tonnes and was powered by a Cummins NTE370 engine. The truck was fitted with Foden FF20 rubber rear suspension. A Foden 8×4 rigid/drawbar trailer unit won the previous award in 1980, while the 1979 award was won by a Foden 6×4 tractor–trailer

unit. All were fitted with the cavernous, locally built Santini cab.

After Foden UK was taken over by Paccar in 1980 Fodens SA was sold to the local management. From then on Foden sales in South Africa declined and within a few years virtually none were sold. In Foden's SA heyday, which was during the 1970s, approximately 350 units were sold annually. Foden operators faced severe problems because parts were very hard to obtain. As a result, older vehicles were cannibalised to keep the rest of the fleet going. It is clear that Foden's reputation was badly affected by this. The existing plant was also outdated and it became obvious the new management was not able to change

things radically. That is why so few S10 Mark 2- and Mark 3-cabbed Fodens were sold in the first half of the 1980s. In August 1986 the inevitable happened: Fodens SA went into liquidation.

Below: Fodens SA was sold to the South African management after Paccar took over Foden in 1980. One of the few Fodens that went into service with South African operators in the early to mid-1980s was a S106T heavy haulage tractor unit, which was powered by a Cummins NTE400 engine. The 100-ton gross tractor unit is coupled to a Hyster four-axle low-loader and was delivered in 1985. It had a S10 Mark 3 sleeper cab fitted with a split windscreen. *(Author's collection)*

Sure Group

In 1985 a company called Sure Parts was established in South Africa. It was set up to sell truck parts at realistic prices. The Sure Group, which owned subsidiary Sure Parts, ran a material handling division that sold, hired and maintained Lansing, NYK and Mitsubishi forklifts.

It also operated a transport and truck rental company. After laborious negotiations with Paccar, which started in early 1987, it was finally agreed Sure Parts would be allowed to distribute Kenworth and Foden trucks in the republic and South-West Africa (now Namibia). Paccar wanted to be convinced that Sure Parts would be able to represent both truck makes in South Africa.

Below: After Fodens SA went into liquidation in 1986, the Sure Group became Foden's representative in South Africa from September 1987 onwards. One of the first sales was this striking 4000 series S106T-4400 tractor unit, fitted with the new S10 Mark 4 cab. It was powered by a locally built Atlantis 422TI-380 engine and photographed when new in 1988 in front of the breathtaking 1,086m high Table Mountain in Cape Town. *(Author's collection)*

Left: S106T-4400 model, dating from around 1990. The double drive tractor unit and South African-built four-axle low-loader was photographed in the yard of Mammoet Kew at Bramley, Johannesburg, in November 1997. Mammoet Kew was a subsidiary of the well-known Dutch Van Seumeren Group. It was a result of a takeover of two South African heavy haulage specialists, Fraser and Kew. *(Lex Meeder)*

Below left: Stuttaford Van Lines of Cape Town had been a loyal Foden operator for decades and was one of the final clients for a new tractor unit in 1991. This S104T-4400 tractor unit, fitted with Atlantis 442TI-360 engine and S10 Mark 4 cab, pulls two special removal trailers. They have large side doors and loading ramps to get easy access. Stuttaford is South Africa's largest and oldest removals company, which was founded in 1857. *(Author's collection)*

It was obvious that it did not want a repeat of the previous bad experiences with the former Foden's SA management. Sure Parts made a successful offer to satisfy Fodens SA's creditors and took over the Foden business in September 1987. The first aim of the new Fodens SA (Pty) Ltd was to provide operators of ageing Fodens with new parts again and secondly to reintroduce Foden to the South African market. Service centres were re-established at Johannesburg, Durban, Port Elizabeth and Cape Town. Both Foden and Kenworth would be assembled at recently commissioned premises in Epping, Cape Town.

It was decided to market the new 4000 series Fodens, which were successfully introduced in the UK in April 1987. They arrived in South Africa in c.k.d. units and the first vehicles were assembled in early 1988. Locally made fuel tanks, tyres, bull bars and other equipment was fitted during assembly. The assembled Fodens would be powered by locally built Atlantis Diesel Engines (ADE), which were in fact licence-built Mercedes–Benz V8 engines. The ADE 422Ti engine developed 380bhp, while the 442T produced 360bhp. It was also possible to import complete vehicles, which could be powered by Cummins engines. Fuller transmissions and Rockwell rear axles completed the drivelines. The new Fodens were launched in June 1988 at all Sure Parts outlets.

In the first year Sure Parts sold thirty-five Fodens, which was about 2 per cent of the South African 20 tonnes and above market. Six of them went into the Sure Group's own haulage and truck rental fleet, Rent-a-Rig Transport. Sure Parts directors believed the Foden 4000 series would be liked by South African operators because they had strong, American style chassis and comfortable European composite cabs. The best-selling Fodens were S106T-model 6×4 tractor units, which weighed around 8 tons, nearly 2.5 tons less than some German competitors. However, the rigid eight S108 models were also on offer, while a little later S104T 4×2 tractors were added to the Sure Parts catalogue. Some of the produced vehicles were exported to neighbouring countries, including Zimbabwe, Botswana and Zambia.

Sure Parts expected to sell around fifty to seventy-five units a year from 1989 onwards. German manufacturers such as Mercedes–Benz and MAN dominated the South African market at the time, although the other Sandbach-based truck manufacturer, ERF, was also well represented. Around fifty vehicles were sold in 1989 but in later years sales declined. In 1990 the new 2000 series Foden was also launched in South Africa but it is not known if any of these 16-tonne rigids were sold there. After some years of promising sales Sure Parts was not able to compete against the American and European opposition any more and sales gradually declined until the assembly and import of Fodens ceased in 1993. In the next decade only two or three new Fodens entered South Africa, imported by the Paccar organisation.

Zimbabwe and Zambia

Hubert Davies

Both countries were British colonies known as North Rhodesia (now Zambia) and South Rhodesia (now Zimbabwe). Zambia became independent in 1964, while Zimbabwe was established in 1980 after Rhodesian prime minister Ian Smith had unilaterally declared Rhodesia independent in 1970.

The same company controlled the Foden agencies for both countries. Hubert Davies & Co. Ltd was appointed Foden's agent in the late 1940s and had one depot in North Rhodesia (Lusaka) and two in South Rhodesia (Bulawayo and Salisbury). Most Foden vehicles arrived

in wooden crates in c.k.d. form and were assembled in Hubert Davies' new depots in Salisbury and Bulawayo, which were built in 1951.

In 1946 the Saker Bartle Company, based in South Africa, sold no fewer than twenty-five DG6/15 eight-wheelers to the Rhodesian State Railways for transport cattle. However, some of them had quite spartan passenger bodies fitted to transport local workers. They were fitted with Gardner 6LW engines and pulled 10-ton four-wheel drawbar trailers. The cabs, cattle and passenger bodies were built in the customer's own workshops. The impressive livestock truck/trailer combinations could carry 25 tons.

Hubert Davies imported Fodens during the late 1940s and throughout the 1950s and 1960s. Foden S18-cabbed tractor units were popular in Rhodesia in the 1950s but Hubert Davies also sold quite a few S18-cabbed FG6/15

Above: This PVSC6 single deck bus model was operated by Salisbury United in Rhodesia in the 1950s. It built its own bodies on to Foden bus chassis, featuring the elegant Foden front grille panel incorporating the Foden kite and logo. These vehicles carried fifty passengers (or more!), loads of luggage on their roof racks and made most of their mileage on unmade roads. Fleet number 118 was restricted to 35mph. *(Peter Tulloch collection)*

Opposite: Hubert Davies imported this impressive Low Line crane carrier into South Rhodesia in the late 1960s. It had a Jones KL15-30 crane on its back and pulled a drawbar trailer to move the 120ft tall main jib and 30ft tall fly jib sections when the vehicle was in transit. *(Julian Hollinshead collection)*

eight-wheelers. Several of the early S18-cabbed 6×4 dump trucks also found their way to Rhodesia, where George Nolan of Fort Victoria operated them.

Some of these vehicles had to work very hard in harsh conditions, including 610-mile return trips hauling copper concentrate through the extensive heat of the bush in the southern part of the country. Three FGTU8/40 double drive tractor units pulled two-axle semi-trailers and three-axle drawbar trailers loaded with 27.5 tons of this product. Each outfit grossed at 46 tons and was powered by a Gardner 8LW-150 engine. Only one of them had a sleeper cab, which is hard to believe nowadays as these vehicles did three return trips in six days every week. Such a journey took forty-four hours, which meant that there was only four hours left to maintain, repair and fuel the vehicles again within the set forty-eight hours. Each vehicle travelled more than 250,000 miles in three years without major mechanical failures, which was a credit to their rugged design. They transported more than 22,000 tons of copper concentrate during this period.

Heavy FGTU6/30 tractor units and FG5/7.5 rigids were used by the Rhodesian Breweries, delivering its famous Castle Beer to all parts of the country. This brewery was associated with the South African Breweries that marketed beer under the same brand. It also used Fodens in its transport fleet.

The Rhodesia Cement Company used Foden dump trucks in 4×2 and 6×4 axle configurations in its limestone quarries in Colleen Bawn, about 100 miles from Bulawayo. The first one was put into service in January 1952 and was fitted with an adapted S18 cab, while later vehicles had the familiar steel half cab fitted. All vehicles were operated on double shifts of eight hours. The Rhodesian Iron and Steel Commission took delivery of an adapted FG6/24 tipper chassis in 1957. The vehicle was fitted with a dumper type half cab and an 11 cubic yards steel tipper body, which was raised by underfloor mounted, twin hydraulic, rams. Hubert Davies also sold a few Foden Low Line crane carriers, which were fitted with Jones cranes.

Finally, even a number of single deck bus chassis were exported to Rhodesia in the early 1950s. Two vehicles were bodied by Massey Bros of Wigan and exported as complete vehicles. The Wankie Colliery, which used them for transporting its workers to and from the colliery, operated them. The colliery also used quite a lot of Foden tippers. Other Foden bus chassis were sent to Salisbury United in Bulawayo, which built its own bodies. These buses were always overloaded with too many people and their large amounts of luggage on the buses' roofs. Nevertheless, they lasted for ten to twelve years, which is quite an achievement bearing in mind that the roads in Rhodesia in the 1950s were unmade or in a bad state. At least fourteen bus chassis were exported to Rhodesia between 1952 and 1954.

Hubert Davies stopped importing Fodens in 1971 and became an ERF agent later.

South African Imports

After Fodens SA had opened its assembly plant in Alberton, vehicles destined for neighbouring countries were assembled in South Africa. They were exported to Rhodesia and some other countries in the area. Political problems and international boycott measures imposed on Ian Smith's government was another reason to import vehicles from neighbouring South Africa, which also had a government ruled by whites at the time. Towards the end of the 1970s many South African-built Fodens, fitted with the South African-built long distance cab, could be seen in Rhodesia. They were operated in the colours of Swift, Clan and North Eastern Transport, to name a few.

Below: Railway Design of Rhodesia built these locomotive style cabs on Foden chassis, which were imported from South Africa. This particular 4×2 tractor unit, pulling two boxvan semi-trailers, was operated by the Rhodesian branch of Stuttaford Van Lines. Fleet number 544 has a top sleeper accommodation for the removal crew. The vehicle dates from 1980 and was photographed in 1985. It is most likely a 4AC29/40 model, powered by a Cummins NTCE290 engine (*D.A. Child*)

Left: Fleet number 506 is another Foden vehicle fitted with a Railway Design cab, featuring a forward sloping windscreen. It was operated by the RMS road transport branch of South Rhodesian Railways. This rigid eight-wheeler has an open top body and pulls a two-axle drawbar trailer. The 8C6 model dates from 1978 and was powered by a Cummins engine. *(Author's collection)*

Right: Clan Transport, now part of Pioneer Transport, operates from Zimbabwe but has also branches in South Africa. Fleet number 813 pulled an aluminium Zambesi boxvan semi-trailer, which was coupled to a drawbar trailer from the same manufacturer. The outfit dates from the early 1980s. *(Niels Jansen collection)*

Left: A 6AC35/65 model Foden fitted with a locally built cab, which was manufactured by Foden importers Hubert Davies from Bulawayo. It is another early 1980s model, photographed in 1983. *(D.A. Child)*

Bottom left: RMS also operated Fodens fitted with the South African-built cab, which was based on S10 cab panels. This 6AC35/65 model was powered by a Cummins NTE350 engine and could gross at 65 tons. The early 1980s tractor unit pulled a semi-trailer and an additional two-axle drawbar trailer. *(Author's collection)*

Below: North Eastern Transport (NET) from Zimbabwe operated a fleet of 6AC35/65 model tractor units. This 6×4 driven unit was fitted with a South African-built single sleeper cab, which incorporated Fleetmaster headlights, grille panel and indicator lights. Fleet number 4124 dates from 1981 and was powered by a Cummins NTE350 engine. The B-train combination, pulling two semi-trailers, is loaded with three 20ft sea containers. It was operated at gross weights of 65 tons and occasionally beyond that figure. *(Niels Jansen collection)*

A substantial number of the imported Fodens from South Africa were fitted with locally built cabs. The Rhodesians built their own cabs during the late 1970s and early 1980s. The cabs had a railway locomotive appearance and had forward-sloping split windscreens, so it doesn't come as a surprise that they were built by Railway Design of Rhodesia. They resembled the steel Foden S60 cab. Most vehicles were 8×4 rigids that often pulled two- or three-axle drawbar trailers, but 6×4 tractor units were also offered. Quite a lot of these sturdy looking vehicles were operated by a company named RMS. Another company, Thorntons of Zimbabwe, which was part of the large United Transport Group, operated a couple of 100-ton plus, 6×4 heavy haulage tractors fitted with the Railway Design cab.

Angola

This part of the world was formerly known as Portuguese West Africa. Fodens were imported by the Portuguese agent Munhas, which had set up a Poden sales and

Below: This old and battered Poden tipper was photographed in Luanda after it had been parked up quite badly at the roadside. It featured a Portuguese coach-built cab and was most certainly imported by the Munhas company, which was based in Portugal. The vehicle is probably a FG6/7.5 model from the early 1950s as the tipper body shows a plate that it can carry a payload of 8.5 tonnes, while the vehicle's own weight is nearly 6 tonnes. *(John Sanderson collection)*

maintenance depot in Luanda in 1952. Munhas sold Podens fitted with Portuguese coach-built or Foden S18 cabs in small numbers to various operators in Angola. Among them were FG6/15 eight-wheelers, which were delivered from 1953 onwards. Towards the end of the 1960s, Lisbon-based Enromotal took over the Munhas business and was responsible for Poden sales during the 1970s.

Tanzania

Tanzania is another British colony that became independent in 1961.

Some DG-series tractor units and rigid vehicles were exported to a company called NSML in Dar es Salaam just before World War II.

The Tanganyika Portland Cement Co. Ltd, which

Below: These three DGTU6/20 series 4×2 tractor units and one DG6/15 8×4 rigid are for export to Tanzania. Although the vehicles are not fitted with a cab, the front hub rings reveal that they are pre-World War II models. They were sent to a company called NSML in Dar es Salaam and were fitted with Gardner 6LW engines, producing 102bhp at the time. The vulnerable S10 cab parts were packed in wooden crates and secured on the backs of the vehicles to be fitted after arrival in Tanzania. *(John Sanderson collection).*

was a subsidiary of the British Portland Cement Co. Ltd, operated a number of 26- and 35-ton gross Foden dump trucks. These provided the basic materials for a single kiln that produced 140,000 tons of cement annually in the mid-1960s.

Kenya

Fodens were imported into Kenya long before it became independent in 1960. Early R-type diesels, fitted with the square W2 cab, were operated by Roadways (Kenya) Ltd in the early 1930s. The four- and six-wheel rigids often pulled drawbar trailers. One of their activities was carrying post and parcels for the Kenyan Royal Mail.

East African Breweries operated several S18-cabbed FG-type Fodens for delivering beer to its customers during the 1950s.

After the establishment of the Kenyan republic, Kenyan companies stayed loyal to Foden, which had a good reputation in this country. The British Portland Cement Co. also operated a large cement plant in Bamburi, 7 miles north of Kenya's main port, Mombasa. The company was named Bamburi Portland Cement and operated Foden dump trucks from the late 1940s. The first FGD6 type dumpers had S18 cabs fitted and shifted coral limestone, which was used in the production of cement, to the kilns.

Above: This FGD6 dump truck fitted with a standard 9 cubic yard Foden tipper body was purchased in 1956 by the Bamburi Portland Cement Co. from its local agents, Riddoch's Garage of Kisumu. It was still running twenty-three years later between the quarry and the crusher, carrying more than one million tons of coral limestone in that period. The company operated seventeen Foden dump trucks in 1979. About half of that number were purchased in the 1950s. *(David Bloor collection)*

Left: Not many early R-type Fodens were exported to Africa. This 1934 three-axle R6 model, pulling a two-axle drawbar trailer fitted with single wheels, is about to unload a large wooden crate, which was delivered in Mombasa by SS *Llandaff Castle*. This ship was built in 1926 and provided a regular service to Kenya. It was hit by two torpedoes fired from a German U-Boot on 30 November 1942 when sailing near the coast of Mozambique. All but three of the 313 passengers and crew survived. The Gardner 6LW-powered vehicle was operated by Roadways (Kenya) and was probably also involved with the transportation of the post as it has a mail crest on the door. *(Author's collection)*

Left: The bucket of this Ruston Bucyrus excavator certainly overloads this little Foden dump truck heavily, but it could handle this abuse quite easily. The East African Portland Cement Co. put it into service during the late 1950s at its Athi River plant in Kenya. A four-cylinder Foden FD4 Mark 3 two-stroke engine, producing 100bhp, powered KFV275. *(Author's collection)*

Right: Fitted with the export version of the S36 cab, this S37-cabbed 6×4 tractor unit pulls a two-axle bottom discharge cement trailer. The 6AXB6/32 model dates from 1969 and was operated by Bamburi Portland Cement of Mombasa. It was powered by a Gardner 6LXB-180 engine. *(John Sanderson collection)*

The 32-ton gross combinations were put into service in 1969. These vehicles were replaced by Gardner 6LXB-180-powered S80-cabbed 6×4 tractor units ten years later, pulling the same type of semi-trailers.

Mozambique

When this country was still a Portuguese colony it operated some very special Foden vehicles. In 1947 four DG6/7.5 tractor units came into the country. They pulled passenger-carrying semi-trailers for the Mozambique Railways. At the same time it took delivery of four DG6/12 six-wheel lorry chassis, which had bus bodies fitted. All eight vehicles also carried goods. In addition, Mozambique Railways ordered another thirty-eight Foden trucks.

In 1953 Foden built and adapted eight 6×4 FG6/12 truck chassis to operate as buses in Mozambique. Massey Bros of Wigan built the bodies, which had compartments for six first class and forty-seven second class passengers. The bus roofs were provided with ample luggage racks. They were shipped to Mozambique in 1954 and put into service by the Lourenco Marques Division of the Mozambique Railways.

Above: The Lourenco Marques Railways in Mozambique took delivery of eight Foden buses in 1954. They were based on normal FG6/12 truck chassis and adapted for bus applications to operate under harsh conditions. The bodies were constructed by Massey Bros of Wigan. They had compartments for six first class and forty-seven second class passengers. They also had ample luggage storage on the roof rack. The vehicles were powered by Gardner 6LW engines and fitted with single tyres all around. *(Peter Tulloch collection)*

Above: Bamburi Portland Cement put this powder tanker into service in 1979. It was a replacement for a ten-year-old S37-cabbed 6×4 tractor unit. The vehicle was based in Mombasa and fitted with a S80 cab and Gardner 6LXB-180 engine. Model AG18/45 pulled a York trailer fitted with a bottom-discharge cement bulk trailer. It could gross at 45 tons. Bamburi Cement is Kenya's leading cement industry, which is now part of the large French Lafarge Group. *(Fodens Ltd)*

At the end of the 1960s the Bamburi Portland Cement kilns had an annual capacity of 700,000 tons at full production. It operated twelve Foden dump trucks in 1969 and even the first one, manufactured in 1947, was still earning its keep. This vehicle was one of the first dump trucks to be built and before it was exported in second-hand state to Kenya, it was used in Wales at a major water project. The heaviest dump trucks grossed at 35 tons and carried 24-ton payloads. Some of these vehicles were still working very hard in the 1980s.

Besides the dump trucks, Bamburi Portland cement also operated some S37-cabbed 6×4 tractor units, which pulled two-axle bottom discharge cement bulk trailers.

Nigeria

Foden was present in Nigeria from the late 1950s. Many Foden FGD-type dump trucks worked on road construction jobs for Costain (West Africa) but other Costain dump trucks earned their keep by moving large pieces of single rock, which weighed anything between 14 and 18 tons, for a major water project. These vehicles worked very hard throughout the 1960s. BP Air operated Foden FG6/20 airfield refuellers at Kano airport during the 1960s.

There were also quite a few Fodens sold in this former British colony during the 1970s. Foden had two agents at the time, one based in Kano and the other in Lagos. The Oshinowo Bus Company ordered seven left-hand drive bus chassis in 1973. They were bodied in the UK by Strachans of Southampton on adapted truck chassis. The vehicles had two-doorway bodies, which accommodated fifty people and were used for city passenger services in what was then the capital city, Lagos. The model 4C6/16 vehicles had Cummins NHK220 engines, which were coupled to a nine-speed gearbox.

Petra Monk Engineering, based in Lagos, took

Above: A RC25/30 model tipper is shown here, ready for export to Nigeria. It was one of ten 30-ton gross tippers that were delivered in 1975 to Petra Monk Engineering based in Lagos for a major road construction contract. The chassis were fitted with steel S41 cabs, heavy bull bars, and steel tipper bodies with strong cab protection canopies. They were powered by trustworthy Cummins NHC250 engines. *(Fodens Ltd)*

Left: This is one of seven bus chassis that were bodied by Strachans Ltd of Southampton in 1973. The rather simple bodies with seating capacity for fifty people featured left-hand drive and sliding side windows. The 4C6/16 model chassis were delivered to the Oshinowo Transport Services Ltd in Nigeria. Cummins NHK220 engines, coupled to nine-speed gearboxes, provided ample power for passenger transport within the capital city of Lagos. *(Fodens Ltd)*

Left: ARC Nigeria was rewarded with a road construction contract in Nigeria in 1975. It ordered several Foden 6×4 tractor units and 6×4 tippers fitted with S41 cabs, which had Cummins 14-litre NHC250 engines under their bonnets. The model AC25/60 Foden tractor units pulled brand new low-loaders or mobile stone crushers including TU8, which was parked up at the port of Lagos. From there they made the 1,100km trip to Bauchi, which is in north-east Nigeria. *(Julian Hollinshead)*

Right: Super Haulmasters were a popular choice with Nigerian contractors in the 1970s. These 1977 RC29/38 model tippers could handle 38-ton gross weights thanks to their large Edbro steel tipper bodies. Steel S90 day cabs, featuring sturdy front bumpers and double headlamps, accommodated powerful Cummins NTCE290 engines. Quite a few were exported by Foden distributors Greenwoods Commercial Vehicles Ltd based in Oxford and Hoddesdon. *(Fodens Ltd)*

delivery of ten 6×4 heavy duty tippers in 1975. They were fitted with steel tipper bodies, which had heavy canopies fitted to protect the drivers from injuries. The steel S41 day cabs were fitted with bull bars. Some of the Cummins NHC250-powered tippers pulled two-axle drawbar trailers, which were also fitted with tipping bodies. Petra Monk also took delivery of a 6×4 tractor unit for heavy haulage applications.

In the 1970s many 38-ton gross Super Haulmaster tipper and 60-ton heavy haulage tractor chassis fitted with steel S90 cabs were exported to Nigeria, many times in conjunction with drawbar- and semi-trailers.

Finally, a Nigerian cement company bought three 4000 series 6×4 tractor units fitted with day cabs in 1997. The Cummins M11.340-powered tractor units pulled 40ft flatbed trailers for West Africa Portland Cement to distribute bagged cement.

Ghana

Ghana became independent in 1957 and was formed by a union between the former Gold Coast and Ghana. These territories were both governed by the British in

Above: Between 1957 and 1961 the Ghana Government Electrical Department took delivery of several FG4/13 chassis fitted with S18 and later with S20 cabs. They carried Butterfield 1,500-gallon tanks to transport fuel. This vehicle is fitted with the tropical version of the S20 cab, featuring a double insulated roof to keep the heat out as much as possible. The vehicles had Gardner 4LW engines fitted, which produced a modest 75bhp. *(John Sanderson collection)*

Left: One of two OG3/4 models that were delivered in 1935 to Bibiani (1927) Ltd, gold mine explorers based in Gold Coast. Foden also sold matching 3-tonne drawbar trailers to the company. The little trucks were powered by a very modest Gardner 3LW diesel engine, producing only 48bhp. The cargo is being unloaded by hand, watched by a colonial supervisor, while the driver is waiting until this job is finished. *(John Sanderson collection)*

the past, but became the new Commonwealth country of Ghana. Foden vehicles were operated in both countries from the late 1940s. The Ashanti Goldfields Co. Ltd took delivery of three FGTU6/20 tractor units fitted with S18 cabs in 1949. They pulled two-axle flatbed semi-trailers. In the same year, three Foden FG4/7.5 type 4×2 rigid vehicles, fitted with Butterfield 1,500-gallon gas oil tanker bodies, were delivered to the Gold Coast Government Electrical Department.

Later, S18-cabbed FG4/13s were delivered to the Ghana Government Electrical Department, which also incorporated the Gold Coast department after 1957. Foden's agent, Paterson Simons & Co. in Accra, delivered more Foden tankers to the same customer in 1961, this time fitted with double roof S20 cabs. The chassis were again fitted with Butterfield 1,500-gallon tanks.

The Consolidated African Selection Trust, which explored opencast diamond sites in Ghana and Sierra Leone, operated many Foden dump trucks. In 1967 it had forty-five Foden dump trucks at work that were powered by Gardner or Rolls–Royce engines. Ashanti Goldfields Corporation was another Foden operator in Ghana, owning and operating several dump trucks during the 1960s and 1970s.

Swedru Contractors Ltd, based in Accra, became a Foden agent for the region in 1976. It was appointed factory representatives for West Africa, which included Ghana, Nigeria, Sierra Leone, Togo, Benin, Liberia and Ivory Coast.

Sierra Leone

Foden vehicles were present in this small West African country from the early 1950s. Forest Industries, based in inland Kenema, operated several heavy FETU6/40, double drive tractor units. They were coupled to two-axle pole trailers and had to work in arduous conditions, particularly during the rainy season. The powerful FD6 Mark 2 two-stroke engines dragged the tractor–trailer combinations through deep forest tracks to take huge trunks to the sawmills.

The biggest Foden customer in Sierra Leone was the Sierra Leone Selection Trust Ltd (SLST), which operated opencast diamond mines at Yengema and Tongo from

1934. The diamond fields were eighty miles apart. In the early 1960s SLST operated several Foden 4×2 and 6×4 dump trucks to transport gravel containing diamonds for washing and screening in SLTS's treatment plants. They also removed any waste material that came free after screening. By 1968 the company already operated thirty-three Foden dump trucks. Five more were added in the same year. These 6D6/30 6×4 dump trucks had Gardner 6LX-150 engines, ten-speed gearboxes, extra heavy duty four-spring rear bogies and were fitted with Neville aluminium alloy tipping bodies that could handle payloads of 23 tons.

Two Foden heavy haulage tractors were used for the transportation of the company's Caterpillar D85 crawler tractors, Ruston Bucyrus RB38 draglines and other plant.

Above: A mid-1950s 6×4 timber tractor is making its way on a rutted African forest track. The tractor unit is a FETU6/40 model, powered by a Foden FD6 Mark 2 two-stroke engine, producing 126bhp. The pole trailer is loaded with huge trunks destined for the saw mills. The vehicle was operated by Forest Industries of Kenema in Sierra Leone. *(David Bloor collection)*

Sometimes transport was provided for other companies by moving diesel-engined railway locomotives. The first tractor was a 1959 model FRHT6/80. This double drive tractor unit was fitted with an S20 cab and powered by a Rolls–Royce C6NFL engine, which developed 210bhp. It was fitted with a replacement S21 cab in 1965.

Left: Sierra Leone Selection Trust (SLST) operated diamond mines in this small African state. It was one of the biggest customers of Fodens in this part of Africa. It operated many Foden dump trucks, but also some heavy haulage outfits to move large pieces of equipment, such as Caterpillar crawler tractors and Ruston Bucyrus dragline excavators. Occasionally it also moved railway stock. This was the first Foden heavy haulage tractor unit, which was purchased in 1959. The FHRT6/80 model was powered by a Rolls–Royce C6NFL engine, producing 210bhp. It pulled a Dyson J-type semi-trailer, which had a payload of 43 tons. *(Author's collection)*

Opposite: One of the FRD6/30 dump trucks that were operated by the SLST in the mid-1960s. They had powerful Rolls–Royce C6N-210 engines and could gross at 30 tons. This one is loaded by a Ruston Bucyrus 38RB dragline. The diamond-containing soil was transported to the washing and screening plants and could involve 20-mile return journeys. *(David Bloor collection)*

Right: The second Foden tractor unit was purchased by SLST in 1965. This 6AX6/76 model is coupled to a J-type Dyson low-loader, which has a Ruston Bucyrus 38RB tracked excavator on its load bed. It is striking that the 38RB is loaded sideways and still has its boom erected, which indicates that the 38RB was moved only over a short distance. The Foden–Dyson outfit could load 43 tons and was powered by a Gardner 6LX-150 engine. A Darlington type 70 winch was mounted behind the S21 cab. *(David Bloor collection)*

FODEN EXPORT VEHICLES

Above: Two early 1960s fully loaded FGD6/30 dump trucks. These very capable dump trucks were powered by Gardner 6LX-150 engines. They worked at the Yengema and Tongo SLTS fields, which were 80 miles apart. *(David Bloor collection)*

The second 6×4 tractor unit, a 1965 model 6AX6/76, had a fibreglass S21 cab fitted. A Gardner 6LX-150 engine, Foden twelve-speed gearbox and double reduction hubs propelled the rear axles. Both vehicles had double roofs for keeping the heat out as much as possible. They both pulled Dyson "J" type semi-trailers and had Darlington winches with a pulling power of 50,000lb mounted behind the cabs.

Egypt

Foden's Egyptian agent, W. Hart, was based in Cairo from the mid-1950s. Another company, Misr–Alexandria General Trade Co. of Alexandria, was Foden's representative in the 1960s. Small numbers of Foden products, mostly dump trucks, were exported to this huge country in the north-eastern part of Africa during the 1970s.

Right: This two-axle dump truck was seen in Egypt during the 1990s. It is obvious that this vehicle has had a rough life as it is quite rusty, battered and is missing some parts, including the front and rear axle mudguards. *(Author's collection)*

Libya

The Indian Road Construction Corporation Ltd ordered eight six-wheel tipper chassis and three six-wheel tanker chassis in 1978. They worked on a road construction programme in Libya, which was awarded to this Indian-based company by the Libyan government. The six-wheel tippers had Gardner 6LXB-engines, S80 Mark 2 cabs and were fitted with steel tipper bodies and Edbro front-end single ram tipping gear. The 38-ton gross Super Haulmaster tankers had S90 steel cabs, Cummins NTCE290 engines and Whale 4,700-gallon water tanks.

Above: The Indian Road Construction Corporation Ltd operated three S90-cabbed 38-ton Super Haulmasters in a road construction scheme in Libya in the late 1970s. The RC29/38 models were built in 1978 and powered by Cummins NTCE290 engines. They had Whale 4,700-gallon tanker bodies fitted, which were used for water transport. *(Fodens Ltd)*

Algeria

The first Foden that landed in Algeria was a drop sided DG6/15 model. It arrived in January 1947 at Bone seaport and was waited for at the quayside by the new owner, Mr Evendon. Foden chassis number 25588 was used for transporting tobacco and other commodities to and from Tunisia and Morocco.

In 1975 five airfield refuellers were built by Gloster Saro on Foden running gear and cab parts. These twin-steer tankers could carry 38,000 litres of fuel and pulled two-axle drawbar units, which had a capacity of 37,000 litres. They were powered by Cummins NHC250 engines coupled to a Brockhouse torque converter and Foden eight-speed gearbox. The low-mounted cab was derived from the S51 dump truck cab, but was built in a full-width version. This cab was designated S53. All vehicles were delivered to Sonatrach, the national oil company of Algeria.

Below: One of five airfield refuellers that were built by Gloster Saro on Foden running gear and cab parts (cab designation S53). They were delivered to Sonatrach, the national oil company of Algeria. The vehicle is running on trade plates and is seen in a British harbour to be shipped to its destination in Algeria. *(Julian Hollinshead)*

Morocco

One or two heavy haulage tractor units were exported to Morocco in the 1970s. The Seferif company operated a S41-cabbed double drive tractor unit in this North African country.

Below: This impressive heavy haulage tractor, pulling a "swan neck" King low-loader, was already painted in the operator's bright yellow livery before it was shipped to Morocco. Seferif purchased this left-hand drive, S41-cabbed, AC25/60 model Foden in 1974. It could gross at 60 tons and was powered by a Cummins NHC250 engine. *(Author's collection)*

CHAPTER FOUR

Exports Asia - Middle East

Cyprus[1]

Foden dump trucks were exported to Cyprus during the 1970s. Kaisis Engineering Ltd of Nicosia was the Foden agent on this sunny Mediterranean Island, situated opposite the Turkish and Syrian coasts.

The Medcon company operated some 6×4 off/on road trucks, which were fitted with locally built cabs. These vehicles were normally fitted with the steel S51 half cabs. Cummins NHK220 engines powered the model 6C6/28 tippers, which could gross at 28 tons.

Nicosia-based Makris Lime operated two 4×2 FL17 dump trucks fitted with half cabs and powered by Leyland EO680 engines, which produced 180bhp. These two vehicles transported excavated lime to the crusher complex.

Other dump trucks were sold to operators such as the Cyprus Cement Co. and Cyprus Asbestos Mines Ltd. Some other Foden trucks were put into service with the Hellenic Mining Co., which operated under the name

Right: This 6C6/28 model on/off-road dump truck was operated by Nicosia-based Medcon construction company. The vehicle had a full-width, locally built cab, which replaced the original steel S51 half cab. It was photographed in Medcon's yard in 1993, already more than twenty years old. The 28-ton gross tipper had a Cummins NHK220 engine installed. *(Peter Seaword)*

Right: Although photographed in Cyprus it is obvious that this eight-wheeler was operated previously by Murphy Bros of Leicester as a tipper. The early 1960s FG6/24 was sold to Cyprus and converted into a crane carrier by adding a small crane and stabilisers. The jib rested on the vulnerable S21 cab during transit. *(David Bloor)*

---

[1] Cyprus belongs geographically to Asia, but most people consider it to be a European island as there is a firm political, social and economic influence from Europe. Cyprus became a member of the European Union in 2004.

Left: Kaisis Engineering Ltd distributors made Foden dump trucks popular in the Greek part of Cyprus during the 1970s. This FC17 dump truck is being loaded in a very dusty environment by a tracked shovel. A Cummins NHK205 engine powered the 1974 model. *(Fodens Ltd)*

Right: The Super Haulmaster range was specifically designed for the export market. They were extremely popular in the Middle East. This RC29/38 model dating from 1978 was operated not far away. The Cyprus vehicle was powered by a Cummins NTCE290 engine and fitted with a German-built Putzmeister "Elefant" concrete pump. The vehicle could gross at 38 tonnes on three axles. A bonneted MAN concrete mixer can be seen in the background. *(David Bloor collection)*

Vassiliko Cement and the Cyprus Building & Road Construction Corporation Ltd.

Turkey

As Foden had an Istanbul-based agent in the 1950s, it is very likely some Fodens were sold in this country. But it took until 1977 before a Turkish based company placed a major order. On the day that the new Foden Fleetmaster and Haulmaster range was introduced in London on 3 November 1977, the Turkish Bahattin Goren organisation ordered no fewer than sixty Super Haulmasters. The vehicles were destined to work on an irrigation project for the Iraqi government. Foden supplied the vehicles in a package deal in which other British manufacturers were also involved. It would supply the necessary bodies, semi-trailers and ancillary equipment. The order consisted of three-axle rigid vehicles for 38-ton gross weight operations and three-axle tractor units, which could gross at 65 tons. The fitted bodies included tippers, concrete mixers and water tankers, while the semi-trailers were low-loaders and 1,200 cu ft bulk cement tankers. All vehicles were fitted with steel S90 cabs, produced by Motor Panels of Coventry.

Syria

The Damascus-based Foden agent, Dr Seif el Dine Tabbakh, was appointed in 1955 and would also represent Foden in Lebanon and Jordan. It is not known how many Fodens it sold during the short representation in the late 1950s, but it probably wasn't many. The agent started well by selling an impressive left-hand drive FE6/15 model rigid eight. It was fitted with an all-metal S18 cab and open top wooden body, which could be covered with a tarpaulin. The driver was lucky in having a bunk fitted in the converted S18 double roof cab and he could even listen to Arabic songs on his radio. The cab's roof was insulated and fitted with a sun visor. It also had an extended chassis fitted with a large steel front bumper, incorporating a strong pulling jaw. Foden's own FD6 Mark 1 six-cylinder two-stroke engine powered this nice looking

Left: The Middle East was by far the biggest market for Super Haulmaster tractor units and rigids in the 1970s. A big order for sixty vehicles destined for the Turkish Bahattin Goren company was completed in 1978. This is one of the 65-ton AC29/65 tractor units, which pulls a Metalair bulk cement semi-trailer. They had Cummins NTCE290 engines installed. All vehicles worked on an irrigation scheme for the Iraqi government. *(Fodens Ltd)*

Left: One of the first Fodens that entered Syria was this impressive 1955 FE6/15 rigid eight, which was powered by a Foden FD6 Mark 1 two-stroke engine, developing 126bhp. It featured an all-metal S18 sleeper cab, which had an insulated double roof and an enlarged external radiator for additional cooling. *(Author's collection)*

vehicle, which had an enlarged radiator fitted. The 126bhp strong engine was coupled to a Foden twelve-speed gearbox.

Jordan

The National Car & Trading Co., based in Amman, represented Fodens in this Kingdom from the late 1960s. In the early 1970s the Jordan Economic and Trading Development Company (COMEDAT) was appointed Foden agent. This company was also based in the capital city of Amman. It sold four FC27 dump trucks to Jordanian Phosphate Mines, which was followed by an order for another twelve vehicles in December 1974. The company was engaged in the clearing of overburden in the phosphate mines.

In 1976 four heavy 6×4 tractor units, fitted with steel S41 cabs, were delivered by COMEDAT to the Jordan Cement Company. These vehicles pulled specially designed Herman bulk cement tankers, which could load 35 tons of cement. The combinations were initially operated in a 100-mile radius around Amman, but later they made deliveries to all parts of Jordan.

Israel

It was striking that there were no Foden agents in Israel before the 1980s. Most likely this was due to the successful Foden sales in many Arab countries. It was not very sensible for manufacturers to also sell their products to Israeli customers during those years; Arabic customers would be very offended and in many cases businessmen had to sign contracts that they would not do any business with Israel.

That all changed after Paccar took over Foden in 1980. The Paccar company already sold Kenworth products to Israeli customers. As Foden products contained quite a lot of American parts and knowledge, it was not a surprise to see Fodens working hard in Israel from the mid-1980s onwards. As a matter of fact, Fodens had similar drivelines and suspensions to most Kenworths. The first models that entered Israel in around 1985 were 6×4 tractor S106T units and 8×4 S108R rigids,

which were fitted with Foden's S10 Mark 3 cabs. Some of the tractor units were fitted with high-power Cummins NTE400 engines and most had heavy Trilex wheels. Almost all export cabs for Israel had optional split windscreens fitted as they could be replaced much more cheaply and easily in case of damage, which is not uncommon in the construction industry.

When the 4000 series was introduced, Paccar saw even more opportunities to sell this new range into Israel, especially after the government increased gross weights in the mid-1990s from 48 tonnes to 63 tonnes. There was a big demand for construction vehicles due to the huge housing schemes to accommodate the many immigrants who still entered the country during the 1990s. Vehicle combinations, having at least seven axles, were allowed to gross at these generous weight limits. This resulted

Opposite: Not only tractor units found their way to Israel. This mid-1980s, Caterpillar-powered, heavy rigid eight pulls a drawbar trailer, carrying demountable bodies on both truck and trailer. The S108 model is fitted with a split windscreen. Broken screens could be replaced easily and cheaply. *(John Sanderson collection)*

Below: The external appearance of this heavy tractor unit gives it an American look, which is enhanced by the Kenworth name on the vehicle's cab side and its Trilex wheels. However, the Foden kite and logo on the grille panel clearly shows its Sandbach origin. The S106T model is fitted with a S10 Mark 3 cab with split windscreen and sits high on its chassis. The Cummins NTE400 powered 6×4 unit was seen parked up on an industrial estate in Eilat in southern Israel in March 1996. *(Richard Tew)*

Left: Another S106T model, working hard at a construction site just north of Tel Aviv. This vehicle has a normal full-width windscreen fitted and is powered by a Caterpillar 3406B-400 engine. It dates from around 1985 and was photographed in March 1996. *(Richard Tew)*

Right: This high capacity oil tanker combination was captured on film at speed in the Negev desert, when it had just left the most southern Israeli port of Eilat. The Caterpillar 3406B-425-powered S108-4450 model was heading towards the Dead Sea area. It dates from 1990 and was photographed in 1996. *(Richard Tew)*

Right: New legislation in the mid-1990s allowed 63-tonne combinations on Israeli roads. This four-axle Foden S108T4-4410 tractor unit pulls a three-axle tipping trailer. The tractor unit has German KHD axles and a Cummins N410 engine fitted. It was encountered on the main coast road just north of Tel Aviv in March 1996. *(Richard Tew)*

Right: Despite being a 4000-series Foden fitted with the S10 Mk5 Hi-Line cab, it is striking that the owners of this 1995 S108R4-4425 model have painted Foden 5000 on the cab sides. The vehicle was fitted with a battered tank body and also showed some damage on the front bumper. The tanker was powered by a big Caterpillar 3406B engine, producing 425bhp. *(Johan Rakels)*

in the use of four-axle tractor units, many of which pulled heavy duty tipping trailers. Foden was one of the manufacturers that delivered them to Israeli customers. In fact, Fodens complemented the Kenworth vehicles as that company had no 8×4 cab-over-engine tractor units available at the time. Foden products were not sold in high numbers in this country. Nevertheless, in the period from 1987 until 2000 quite a few 6×4 rigids, 8×4 rigids, and 8×4 tractor units entered service with Israeli customers. Some of the three- and four-axle drawbar combinations entered service with oil companies. They were fitted with the road-friendly Air-Trac suspension and powered by Cummins N410 engines.

During the late 1990s Kenworth sold bonneted T800 model trucks on the Israeli market, which were assembled at Sandbach. Exports to Israel ceased with the introduction of the Alpha range and the end of 4000 series cab production. Another reason was the strong presence of DAF Trucks, which became a sister company of Foden in November 1996. DAF was very successful in Israel with its 95-series model, which was also available in four-axle tractor unit specification.

Iran

The British-based construction company Marples Ridgway Ltd was awarded a major road building contract in Iran in 1975. The 300km road project was planned in the south-east part of the country, near the Pakistan border. It was not only a matter of road construction, but it also involved the construction of bridges and culverts. More than 4 million cu m of earth had to be removed. Marples Ridgway ordered no fewer than forty Foden vehicles to complete the job. The vehicles were exported to Iran towards the end of 1975 and consisted of twenty-five six-wheel tippers fitted with steel tipping bodies, S41 day cabs and left-hand drive. Another 6×4 vehicle also had an S41 day cab, but this vehicle was fitted with a Drillmaster A60 hydraulic rotary drill, which was manufactured and fitted to the chassis by Hands–England Drilling Ltd of Letchworth. The rest of the order consisted of eleven six-wheel dump trucks and three four-wheelers, all fitted with the familiar half cab.

Above: In 1975 UK-based Marples Ridgway constructors was awarded a contract to build a 300km road in Iran near the Pakistan border. It ordered twenty-five of these heavy RC25/30 tipper chassis, which were powered by Cummins NHC250 engines. Gross weight of these left-hand drive S41-cabbed vehicles was 30 tonnes. *(Julian Hollinshead collection)*

Below: Sam Whan Enterprises, a construction company based in South Korea, operated several Foden tractor units and dump trucks for a contract near the Saudi Arabian capital of Riyadh. This is one of two 6×4 tractor units fitted with left-hand drive S41 day cabs and powered by Cummins NHC250 engines. The AC25/60 model was built in 1974 and was coupled to a Dyson low-loader. *(Dyson Trailers)*

Saudi Arabia

Sam Whan Enterprise Co. Ltd, based in Seoul (South Korea), placed an order for two left-hand drive 6×4 tractor units in 1974. The Cummins NHC250-powered vehicles were exported to Saudi Arabia in conjunction with two Dyson semi-trailers, one being a low-loader and the other a flatbed. Both vehicles were fitted with steel S41 day cabs. The vehicles assisted in

environmental projects near Riyadh. This company also operated fourteen Foden FC17 two-axle dump trucks.

Three years later the British-based Fives Lille Cail (UK) of Surrey won a large contract to set up a new quarry plant in Saudi Arabia. In order to fulfil the contract it ordered twelve Foden AC25/60 double drive tractor units pulling two-axle semi-trailers fitted with steel tipper bodies. The Anglo–French company also ordered two FC27 three-axle dump trucks. The

Below: British-based Foster Yeoman ordered a large batch of 36-ton Super Haulmaster tippers in 1977. The RC29/36 tipper chassis had steel S90 day cabs fitted and 16.5 cu m Edbro-built steel tipper bodies. They had optional Trilex wheels and were powered by Cummins NTCE290 engines. *(Author's collection)*

Left: However, a few of the 36-ton gross weight vehicles delivered to the Fairclough–Al Midani consortium were fitted with personnel-carrying bodies. These vehicles had S90 steel Motor Panels cabs. They were involved in the construction of airfield sites in the northern part of Saudi Arabia. *(Author's collection)*

Below: This is one of nearly sixty Super Haulmasters that delivered to the British–Saudi Arabian consortium Fairclough–Al Midani in 1977. The RC29/36 models had Cummins NTCE290 engines fitted and were operated in water or fuel tanker, concrete mixer or tipper configurations. *(Fodens Ltd)*

tractor–trailer combinations travelled overland to the French port of Marseille, where they picked up the quarry plant parts and equipment. They then embarked a roll-on, roll-off vessel to travel to the Red Sea port of Jeddah. From there the vehicles had to travel more than 1,000km before they reached their final destination, the quarry location at Al Hufuf. The 40-ton payload tipper combinations, fitted with S41 day cabs and powered by Cummins NHK250 engines, were also used for hauling aggregates to customers within a 100-mile radius of the quarry.

In the same year Foster Yeoman ordered a large batch of 6×4 on/off-road Super Haulmaster tipper chassis, which were fitted with 20 cu m steel tipper bodies, manufactured by Edbro UK. The 36-ton gross weight tippers had steel S90 cabs fitted and were powered by 14-litre Cummins NTCE290 engines. The twenty-one vehicles operated at a limestone quarry in Saudi Arabia that was developed by the British-based company. As they were fitted with 12.00-24 tyres fitted on Trilex wheels they could handle payloads of at least 23 tons, but in the quarries they regularly took much more weight. Some of the tippers were later converted into tractor units to deliver the crushed limestone to the quarry's customers.

A British–Saudi Arabian consortium called Fairclough–Al Midani operated the largest fleet of Fodens in Saudi Arabia. No fewer than thirty-eight Super Haulmaster 6×4 rigids and nineteen Super Haulmaster 6×4 tractor units entered the country in 1977. The S90-cabbed vehicles were involved in the construction of airfield sites in the north. The 38-ton 6×4 rigid vehicles were fitted with concrete mixers, tipper bodies, water and fuel tanks or personnel carrier bodies. Most of the 65-ton gross tractor units pulled bulk cement semi-trailers from the Jeddah harbour to the company's base in Hail. This involved a 1,350km round trip, which normally took twenty-two hours. It took the drivers through hot deserts and the Hejaz mountains. The rest of the Cummins NTCE290-powered units moved heavy plant to and from various locations.

Within four years more than 110 Fodens were operated in Saudi Arabia. Two houses in Damman accommodated Foden sales and service representatives, while other depots were based in Jeddah and Riyadh. Sadly, after Paccar's takeover in 1980 virtually no new Fodens were exported to this large kingdom.

Kuwait

Foden vehicles were operated in this small oil exporting country from the 1950s. The biggest Foden operator was Port Authorities, a government-owned company that ran a fleet of seventy Fodens at the end of the 1950s. The Foden agent, Bader Al Mulla, took its first order in 1953. The first forty-three Foden 20-ton tractor units, fitted with S18 cabs, arrived in early 1954. A Foden works driver spent more than two months instructing the local drivers in driving and maintenance techniques.

Bader al Mulla would represent Foden for twenty years until Mustafa Karam Trading took over the agency in 1972. The Port Authorities' fleet consisted of many FGTU6/25 tractor units, fitted with steel double roof S18 and S20 cabs, Gardner 6LW engines and Foden five-speed gearboxes. It also owned a 1961 FG6/20 6×4 recovery truck fitted with a S20 cab. It was equipped with an 8-ton Harvey Frost slewing type crane and an 80,000lb Darlington capstan winch, which was mounted behind the vehicle's cab.

Above: Kuwait was an important export market for Foden from the early 1950s, when the company took orders for forty-three Gardner 6LW-powered FGTU6/20 tractors units fitted with S18 cabs. Repeat orders came in during the early 1960s, when these FGTU6/25 tractor units, fitted with S20 cabs featuring double insulated roofs, were delivered as replacements. They pulled the same high-sided drop side trailers as the S18s did in 1954. *(John Sanderson collection)*

Bahrain

Many S18- and S20-cabbed Fodens have helped to develop the oil industry in the island of Bahrain, which is situated in the Arabian Gulf, just west of Qatar. The Bahrain Oil Company, which was a subsidiary of Caltex Oil, operated quite a few S18-cabbed 6×4 rigids and tractor units in the 1950s. The FGTU6/40 tractor units pulled semi-trailers fitted with drilling rigs. In erected form they drilled 60ft deep and 4in wide holes, which were filled with explosives. The sensitive instruments recorded whether the underground structures would contain oil or not.

Left: Bahrain Petroleum Company, which was a subsidiary of Caltex Oil, operated many Foden vehicles in the 1950s and 1960s. This FG6/20 oilfield truck was used to lift heavy components at drilling sites near the Arabian Gulf. The 1959 model was equipped with a heavy winch and powered by a Gardner 6LX-150 engine. *(Author's collection)*

Right: Sardar Transport fleet number 50 is pulling a tiny and narrow low-loader to transport a Toyota forklift. The 4AXB6/32 model tractor unit has an export version of the S39 fibreglass cab fitted (S38) and was powered by a Gardner 6LXB-180 engine. *(Author's collection)*

Above: An S41-cabbed 6×4 tractor unit converted into a platform machinery transporter that was operated by A.E. al Nooh based in Bahrain. It has a HAP3 loading crane fitted at the back of the load bed. *(Julian Hollinshead)*

In the 1960s and 1970s, S20-, S21-, S37- and S38-cabbed Fodens were widely used by some local operators, including Al Majid Transport and Sardar Transport. They were worked really hard until they were completely at the end of their lives. Finally, the Ameen Company operated some S83-cabbed tractor units in conjunction with two-axle flatbed semi-trailers.

United Arab Emirates (UAE)

Trucial States

This union of seven sheikhdoms was formerly known as the Trucial States. The British established the Trucial States Council in 1952; previously the area was known as the Pirate Coast. After Britain withdrew from the territories along the Arabian Gulf in 1968, it took a couple of years before the United Arab Emirates was finalised. That took place in 1971, although initially only six sheikhdoms took part in the union. Ras al-

Khaimah joined Abu Dhabi, Dubai, Sharjah, Ajman, Umm al-Quwain and Fujairah later. The UAE can be found just west of the Strait of Hormuz, the gateway to the Arabian Gulf. The country borders Saudi Arabia and Oman.

Oil exploration in the area started in the 1930s and reached a peak in the 1950s. However, the biggest oil reserves had still to be discovered in the early 1960s. Oil was struck on and offshore in enormous quantities in Dubai, Abu Dhabi and Sharjah. These finds caused a big demand for construction equipment to build new harbours for the large oil tankers, but also for the development of the necessary infrastructure on land. A new Foden sales and service agent for the area was appointed towards the end of the 1960s. General Navigation & Commerce Co. Ltd (Genavco), based in Dubai, would represent Foden in the Trucial States, Bahrain, Muscat and Oman.

Genavco

Genavco's first sales in 1968 were several double drive, 6AC6/50 tractor units. The 50-ton gross articulated vehicles were fitted with double roof export versions of the S34 tilt cab. These cabs were designated S35 and were 2.5in narrower than the standard S34. The Cummins NH220-powered tractor units had huge single sand tyres on the rear bogies. They pulled large two-axle flatbed semi-trailers, which also were fitted with single sand tyres of about the same size as the tractor units. In the same year a large batch of 6XB6/24 three-axle tippers, fitted with the same S35 cab and single sand tyres on the rear bogies, arrived in the Trucial States. These 24-ton gross weight vehicles had Gardner 6LXB-180 engines fitted. It was remarkable that Foden issued brochures in the Arabic language featuring these impressive export vehicles.

Right: Foden sales were so successful in Arab countries during the 1960s that the company decided to issue special brochures in Arabic. The Trucial States Foden distributor Genavco distributed this 1969 brochure among potential customers. The front page shows four heavy duty tippers fitted with huge single sand tyres on their rear bogies. The 6XB6/24 models feature S35 fibreglass tilt cabs and Gardner 6LXB-180 engines. *(Author's collection)*

Opposite page: Dubai Port Authority (DPA) took delivery of this heavy 6×4 tractor unit, which was fitted with a fixed S37 cab. It pulled a Fruehauf flatbed semi-trailer. The late 1960s model was sold by Genavco distributors and was most likely powered by a Cummins NHK220 or 250 engine. *(David Bloor collection)*

مركبات نقل مصمادة ثلاثة طراز "فودن" ٦ إكس بي ٦ /٢٤ ٢٤ "FODEN 6XB 6/24" معدة للتصدير إلى منطقة الخليج العربي. مزودة بمحركات "غاردنر GARDNER" ١٨٠ ح.ق.ف. حمولتها الآجرة ١٦ طناً.

FODENS LTD., ELWORTH WORKS, SANDBACH, CHESHIRE, ENGLAND
& 139 PARK LANE, LONDON W.1., ENGLAND

Costain

The British Costain Civil Engineering Ltd was awarded a large contract in 1967 for the construction of Port Rashid in Dubai. The £24 million contract involved the construction of two breakwaters and fifteen berths, which accommodated big ships up to 30ft draughts. The deep water harbour facility was completed in 1972 and it was then the biggest manmade harbour in the Middle East. Foden supplied Costain with ninety vehicles in 1968 to fulfil the job. The order included two-axle 24-ton gross dump trucks and 26-ton three-axle tippers fitted with export versions of the S21 cab. The most impressive vehicles were the huge 40-ton 8R6/40 type 8×4 dump trucks, fitted with large steel tipper bodies raised by Edbro tipping gear, cab protection canopies and set forward half cabs. They had Foden twelve-speed gearboxes fitted and Foden 20-ton rear bogies with double reduction hubs. Other Rolls–Royce 220-powered 8×4 dump truck chassis acted as skip carriers, which accommodated two large skips. The necessary rock was excavated from a quarry some 20 miles from the projected harbour and transported by the Foden tippers and skip carriers to its final destination. Ten years later these machines still worked for Costain, supplying rock to a new harbour project near Jebel Ali, south of Dubai. Many had done more than a million miles and, although badly battered, they still did their jobs.

Above right: Costain, a civil engineering company based in the UK, was awarded a large contract for the construction of Port Rashid in Dubai and ordered ninety Foden dump trucks and tipper chassis. Among them were many heavy 40-ton gross weight 8×4 dump trucks, which were powered by Rolls–Royce Eagle 220 engines. The model 8R6/40 vehicles were delivered to Costain in 1968. This photographs shows one of them when it was new. *(Author's collection)*

Right: One of the Foden 8R6/40 dump trucks at work in Dubai. The Costain vehicles had hard lives, but they did their job for more than ten years at various harbour construction projects. Many had done more than a million miles by the time they were retired. This photograph shows clearly that the vehicles had fixed protection canopies. *(David Bloor collection)*

Booming 1970s

Taylor Woodrow joined forces with Costain in 1974 to create a £91 million dry dock for the sheikh of Dubai. No fewer than thirty-six three-axle FC27 dump trucks were needed to transport rock from a quarry to the construction area in the newly formed United Arab Emirates. Lebanese and Greek companies used quite a lot of Foden FC17 two-axle dump trucks for road construction projects in the UAE. At the same time, eight two-axle Foden FC17 dump trucks were operated on Das Island, about 100 miles off the coast of Abu Dhabi. It would be used as a processing and storage site for oil but before the tanks could be installed the site had

Below: The Dubai Rock Company operated this 1974 FC27 dump truck in a big harbour project. It was one of nearly 450 Foden vehicles imported by Genavco between 1968 and 1978. Genavco and Foden technicians gave the necessary technical after sales support to their customers based in all the emirates.
(Author's collection)

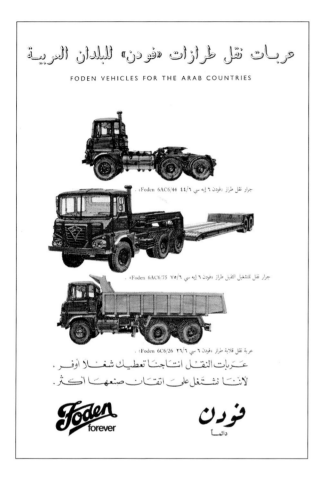

Above: Another special Foden brochure in Arabic that was issued to Middle East customers. It shows the 1970s Cummins-powered Foden truck series fitted with S40 and S41 cabs. The rigid tippers could gross at 26 tons, while the tractor units could handle gross combination weights of 44 and 75 tons.
(David Bloor collection)

Opposite: Eight two-axle Foden FC17 dump trucks were operated by Costain, Tarmac and a Lebanese-based construction company on Das Island in the Arabian Gulf, which is about 100 miles off the coast of Abu Dhabi. Here one of the FC17s is loaded by a tracked shovel, while the flames and smoke of the nearby oil refinery are clearly visible.
(Author's collection)

to be raised by 6m. Costain, Tarmac and a Lebanese-based construction company started the job in 1974 but the Fodens were still at work there in 1978.

In 1976 Foden importer Genavco took delivery of some AC25/60 three-axle tractor units, which pulled three-axle low-loaders to transport heavy construction plant. These vehicles had S41 day cabs fitted, were powered by Cummins NHC250 engines and grossed at 60 tons.

In 1977 the Costain–Taylor–Woodrow consortium ordered twenty AC29/60 three-axle tractor units and two-axle tipper trailers to transport aggregates 60 miles from a quarry in Dubai to the Arabian Gulf. These tractor units had S41 day cabs fitted over the Cummins NTC290 engines. Gross combination weight of these outfits was 63 tons, which created a payload of 48 tons,

Above: The S41 cab, manufactured by Motor Panels, was quite popular in the Middle East. This RC33/34 model had a powerful Cummins NTC335 engine fitted and was designed for a 34-ton gross weight. It was equipped with a steel double roof and sleeper extension. The fitted body was a typical Middle East product, consisting of steel sides, high railings, tarpaulin rack and lots of rope hooks. In practice the 34-ton gross weight was exceeded regularly. It was operated since May 1974 by Mustafa Karam from Dubai. *(John Sanderson collection)*

and the outfits travelled at 55mph. In the same year, the Tarmac Roadstone quarry in Sharjah received thirty-eight Fodens, which were used for hauling aggregates from a quarry in Dhaid. The order consisted of nineteen heavy duty 6×4 tractor units fitted with S41 cabs, nine

Left: A British-registered, early 1960s Foden S20-cabbed tractor unit and tank trailer, which was still operated in the mid-1970s by Tarmac in Dubai. The man on the left is dressed in a typical Arabic desert outfit, while the man on the right most certainly is a sun-loving West European Tarmac employee. *(Julian Hollinshead)*

Right: One of nineteen 6AC6/44 Cummins powered tractor units delivered to Tarmac Roadstone in one of the United Arab Emirates, Sharjah. Most were used for the construction of a highway between Sharjah and Daid, hauling aggregates from a Tarmac quarry in the latter place. This tractor unit pulls a silo trailer that delivered cement for a new sewage works just outside Sharjah. *(David Bloor collection)*

Left: Dubai Transport Co. operated this left–hand drive Super Haulmaster tractor unit that dates from 1979. Fleet number ET107 was an AC29/45 model, powered by a Cummins NTCE290 engine and fitted with a steel S90 (Motor Panels) day cab. The whole combination was designed for a combined gross weight of 45 tons. It pulls a high gravity tipping semi-trailer, which had a body raised by double hydraulic rams. *(David Bloor collection)*

Right: A proud driver stands next to a left-hand drive, S41-cabbed 8×4 tipper operated by Tarmac in Sharjah. The picture was taken in the mid-1970s by Foden service engineer Julian Hollinshead.

Super Haulmaster 6×4 concrete mixers and ten eight-wheel tippers.

Balfour Beatty operated twenty-five three-axle FC27A dump trucks, of which some had been converted into tractor units. The S51-cabbed tractor units pulled heavy duty tipper trailers; the whole outfit was shod with big, single sand tyres. They worked on a harbour project in Jebel Ali together with a yellow fleet of 36-ton Super Haulmaster three-axle tippers and 65-ton three-axle tractor units, pulling Dyson tipper trailers. Both types of the S90-cabbed Super Haulmasters had Cummins NTCE290 engines fitted. The Dubai Transport Company operated them for twenty-four hours a day, seven days a week. They shifted more than 5,000 tons of stone a day over a 75-mile distance.

A number of 6×4 concrete mixer chassis fitted with 8.5 cu m Ritemixer mixer drums were shipped to Dubai in 1978. The mixers were hydraulically driven by a donkey engine. The Super Haulmaster vehicles were fitted with S90 day cabs and delivered to the Al Moosa Tilcon company, which was a joint venture with the British-based Tilling Construction Services (Tilcon). In the same year, a fleet of Super Haulmaster 6×4 tractor units arrived at BP's depot at Sharjah. These tractor units pulled semi-trailers fitted with Hargill 8,000-gallon tanks, which were manufactured in Malaysia. The tanker combinations delivered fuel to aircraft at the local airport as well as to filling stations and industrial users.

In 1978 more than 450 Fodens worked in the UAE, mostly on various construction projects. They gave sterling service to their operators for many years. Genavco and Foden technicians provided the necessary service and after sales.

Schlumberger

It took until the late 1990s before new Fodens entered the UAE again. The American-based Schlumberger engineering group announced a truck concept in 1996, which was based on a single truck manufacturer, namely Foden. The Foden 4000 series was chosen to form the basis for Schlumberger vehicles. A number of these Fodens were badged as Kenworth S106R4 models and were specifically designed to meet the demand for a world oilfield service truck. They complied with European

Above: Schlumberger, the American-based oilfield explorers, operate Foden vehicles all over the world. The S106R4 model was specially designed to meet demand for a world oilfield service truck. This Kenworth-badged Foden is an S106R4-4380 model, powered by an 11-litre Cummins M11-380 engine. Fleet number 2120 has an S10 Mark 5 low roof sleeper cab fitted and was operated by Dowell Schlumberger (Muscat Branch). It was photographed in Oman in 2004. *(Arie van den Brand)*

and US legislation. Paccar combined Kenworth and Foden technology to create a rugged and reliable truck for well logging services. Cummins M11-series engines powered these impressive S106R4 models, which were fitted with a 4000 series low roof cab equipped with a single bunk. Air conditioning equipment was standard, as was a master battery disconnecting switch and an inboard fire extinguisher.

The Schlumberger company is involved with oil exploration engineering jobs all over the world, from the USA to the Middle East. Towards the late 1990s, several Foden 4000 series four-wheel drive vehicles emerged in Abu Dhabi to do their jobs at the oil fields. From 2003 until 2006 the Schlumberger vehicles were fitted with the second generation Alpha cab.

Fodens sold more than 250 vehicles to the

Schlumberger organisation, which were used for its worldwide activities. A fully built up Foden Alpha Mark 2 6×4 rigid, including body and electronic and seismic equipment, would cost around £500,000 each. These chassis were manufactured in left- and right-hand drive to be deployed anywhere in the world.

Right: Foden also built 4×4 models for Schlumberger, which had to operate in difficult off-road conditions. They had smaller bodies fitted, which also featured a Maxis Express imaging system for oilfield surveys. This S104x4R4-4405 model was built in 2000 and is seen at high speed in an Arabian desert. Fleet number 3501 had a Cummins M11.405 engine installed. It shows the latest S10 Mark 5 cab fitted with an Alpha-type grille panel. It had a left-hand drive configuration. *(Foden Trucks)*

Right: When production of the 4000 series ceased, all new Schlumberger vehicles were fitted with Alpha-type cabs. This right-hand drive 6×4 vehicle is fitted with the second generation Alpha 3000 series cab and powered by a Cummins ISM345E engine. It has a four-bag Air-Trac rear suspension and is able to gross at 26 tonnes. *(Foden Trucks)*

Far East

India

Foden steam wagons were exported to India in the 1920s and 1930s. Diesel-powered lorries were present in this former part of the British Empire from the early 1950s. Marshall & Sons & Co. (India) became Foden's agents then with depots in Calcutta, Bombay, New Delhi, a head office in Madras, and a depot in Ceylon.

Foden dump trucks were popular in this huge country. The first FGD6 three-axle models to enter India were fitted with the metal S18 cabs, which were equipped with a tropical double roof. These vehicles had a Gardner 6LW engine, Foden twelve-speed gearbox and 9 cubic yard steel body. The Andhra government operated them on major construction works. It also operated several FGTU6/30 heavy haulage tractor units fitted with double roof S18 cabs, transporting materials and equipment to hydroelectric projects.

Real heavy haulage tractor units also found their way to India. An impressive FGHT8/80 ballasted tractor fitted with an S18 crew cab was imported by Marshall in 1958. The tractor unit had a Gardner 8LW engine fitted, which produced 150bhp. It was coupled to a 50-ton payload Dyson girder trailer, which had four axle rows. The trailer itself weighed a staggering 44 tons. It was destined for the Neyvili Lignite Corporation to move heavy plant. The Madras Public Works Department took delivery of its fourth Foden tractor unit in 1965. The latest addition to its fleet was a heavy duty tractor unit fitted with an S20 day cab.

More dump trucks were delivered to Hindustan Steel in Durgapur in the 1960s. It operated twenty-four Foden two-axle dump trucks in its iron and steel works. Another ten three-axle dump trucks worked hard for many years on the construction of the Farakka Barrage, situated about 200 miles from Calcutta. Five of the 31-

Opposite: This image shows three types of Foden well logging vehicles, which were operated by Schlumberger. From left to right there is a Kenworth-badged 4000 series 6×4, a second generation Alpha 3000 series 6×4 and a 4000 series 4×4, all of which have left-hand drive. The Alpha truck was brand new as it had no registration plates fitted yet. *(Foden Trucks)*

Above: This FGHT8/80 heavy haulage ballast tractor was exported to India in 1958. The Gardner 8LW-150 powered tractor pulled a 50-ton capacity Dyson double cranked trailer, which had four axle rows. It was delivered to the Neyveli Lignite Co. of Madras by Foden's distributor, Marshall & Sons (India), which was also based in Madras. *(Peter Daniels collection)*

ton dump trucks carried clay, while the others carried cement. The barrage provided a road and rail bridge connection over the sacred river Ganges. Another Indian dump truck operator was the Hyderabad Cement Co.. In 1975 Tractors India Ltd became Fodens new agent after Marshall & Sons had represented the company for more than twenty years.

Thailand

The Metropolitan Electrical Authorities, based in Bangkok, took delivery of a 6AC6/75 heavy haulage tractor unit in 1973. The 6×4 tractor unit was powered by a Cummins NHK250 engine, Foden twelve-speed gearbox and a steel S41 day cab. It was used for moving heavy transformers on its three-axle low-loader trailer.

Below: A Foden ballast tractor financed by the Colombo plan that was initiated by seven countries, including Canada and India, in 1950 to enhance social and economic development in Asia and the Pacific. The 1959, S20-cabbed FGHT8/80 tractor was powered by a Gardner 8LW-150 engine. It was shipped to the port of Cochine (Kerela State, India), and driven overland to the Nilgiris district, which is part of the Tamil Nadu State situated in the southern part of India. It moved heavy machinery and other equipment during the construction of six different Kundah Hydro-Electric power houses that were built between 1960 and 1964. *(David Bloor collection)*

Malaysia

Foden exports to Malaysia, or Malaya as it was called then, started in the mid-1950s. They included heavy duty FGTU6/30 and FGTU6/40 heavy haulage tractor units, which were coupled to Dyson-built low-loader trailers in most cases. The tractor units were fitted with steel S18 export cabs and some had Darlington winches mounted behind their cabs, which had a pulling power of 50,000lb.

Foden was still exporting vehicles to this country during the 1960s. These vehicles were operated in road construction and electricity schemes by various government organisations. The Public Works Department (PWD) operated a fleet of S18 and S20 type heavy haulage tractors, which moved equipment from its base in Ipoh (West Malaysia) to development projects all over the country. The S18 tractor unit was still working hard in the mid-1970s. PWD also operated the Bukit Mor Quarry on the west coast of Johor,

Below: British Borneo Timber (BBT) was an early Foden customer that explored forests in British North Borneo. Fleet number 34 was a 100-ton FGHT6/100 model powered by a Gardner 6LX-150 engine. It had to work in difficult circumstances, hence it was fitted with heavy protection equipment for radiator, headlights and engine underside. It also had a huge additional fuel tank fitted just behind the tropical (double roof) version of the S20 cab to supplement the smaller standard fuel tank on the left-hand side of the tractor unit. It pulled a two-axle Crane pole trailer that could be carried on the prime mover when the vehicle was not loaded. *(John Sanderson collection)*

Left: The Public Works Department (PWD) of Malaysia operated this S20-cabbed heavy haulage tractor that moved equipment to development projects all over the country. The model FCHT6/80 dates from around 1960 and was powered by a Cummins NHB6 engine that produced 210bhp. The tractor unit was also fitted with a heavy winch mounted behind the cab. PWD is a government organisation that is more than 100 years old and is responsible for the country's infrastructure. *(Author's collection)*

Right: This battered tractor unit with no doors started life as a FG6/14 dump truck with the Sabah Timber Company based in Sandakan, Malaysia. The early 1960s S20-cabbed dump truck was converted into a tractor unit in 1966. It moved 15 to 20 tons of timber from Lungmanis Camp, over a distance of 15 miles. The company told Foden in a letter that the vehicle gave very little trouble, but was on the slow side (Gardner 6LW-112bhp) and rather heavy on steering. *(David Bloor collection)*

Left: Early 1960s double drive tractor unit coupled to a four-in-line, low-loader semi-trailer. These heavy tractors were fitted with hub reduction axles and could be powered by Gardner, Rolls–Royce, Cummins or Foden two-stroke engines. This one was delivered to the State of Johore in Malaysia. The tractor unit was fitted with a double-skinned tropical roof S20 cab and a heavy winch fitted behind the cab. *(John Sanderson collection)*

Right: One of the FC17 type dump trucks that were operated by the Public Works Department of Johore State in Malaysia well into the 1980s. It is being loaded by a Ruston Bucyrus bucket excavator. *(John Sanderson collection)*

which had an output of 250 tons of crushed stone per hour. PWD operated many Foden FC17 dump trucks well into the 1980s.

Foden dump trucks were operated by various Malayan companies, such as the Gopeng Consolidated Mines, but also by companies in the tin exploration industry, including the Hong Kong Tin Ltd, Petaling Tin, Kinta Kellas Tin, Pengkalen Tin and the Idris Hydraulic Tin Co.

North Borneo, which became part of the Malaysian Federation in the mid-1960s, also operated quite a lot of Fodens, mainly in the logging industry. The Sabah Trading Co. operated S20 type tractor units that pulled four-wheel timber pole-trailers. The tractor units had no doors, despite the fact it rained nearly every day in the humid tropical forests. The trailers handled loads of hardwood timber that weighed 15 to 20 tons. Heavy Foden timber tractors were also exported to British North Borneo in the 1950s and early 1960s. The BBT Company operated several double drive S18 and S20 tractor units, which pulled heavy Dyson pole trailers. These could be carried on the prime mover when the trailer was empty. A Gardner 8LW eight-cylinder diesel engine, which produced 150bhp, powered the S18 type FGTU8/40 tractor units. The S20 type combinations were designed for 100-ton gross combination weights.

Hong Kong

Green Island Cement was one of Foden's oldest customers in this former, densely populated, British Crown colony. It ordered a couple of double drive tractor units in 1966, which were powered by Gardner 6LXB-180 engines, coupled to Foden twelve-speed gearboxes. The tractor units had S35 export type tilt cabs fitted and would pull frameless BTC/Interconsult bulk semi-trailers or logging pole trailers. Green Island Cement also operated three- and four-axle concrete mixers and tractor units fitted with S24 tilt cabs.

The Hong Kong Fire Service took delivery of a 6×4 Foden chassis fitted with a S21 cab and a recovery body in the mid-1960s. The Westminster Plant Co., Flat Hill Quarry and Gammon (Hong Kong) Ltd operated Foden two- and three-axle dump trucks on civil engineering

Above: The Japanese Nishimatsu Company operated several FGD6/26 dump trucks and a FC16 crane carrier in Hong Kong in the 1960s. They were engaged on building the Plover Cove Reservoir in Hong Kong that could hold 170 million cu m of fresh water. The 2km-long dam and reservoir was constructed between 1960 and 1968. The capacity of the reservoir was increased to 230 million cu m in 1973. *(David Bloor collection)*

Below: Green Island Cement operated this 4AX6/25 model tractor unit, which dates from 1965. It was powered by a Gardner 6LX-150 engine and pulls a BTC four-in-line cement bulk trailer. It is fitted with Foden's first tilt cab, designated S24, which was introduced in 1962. The combination is photographed in Sandbach prior to export to Hong Kong. *(John Sanderson collection)*

jobs, such as bridge construction, housing schemes and even the development of the local Shatin racecourse. The Japanese Nishimatsu Construction company operated a Foden crane carrier and several three-axle dump trucks on the Plover Cove scheme, which would supply Hong Kong with additional drinking water.

In 1977 a very special Foden vehicle was shipped to Hong Kong and delivered to the Lion Rock Tunnel Co. This vehicle, an AG18/30 tractor unit model, was

Left: Green Island Cement also operated concrete mixers, such as this 1966 eight-wheel 8X6/24 model, fitted with a S24 tilt cab and powered by a Gardner 6LX-150 engine. Fleet number 802 carries a Rapier concrete mixer. *(Author's collection)*

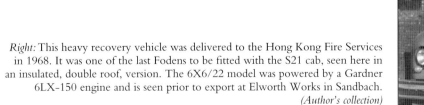

Right: This heavy recovery vehicle was delivered to the Hong Kong Fire Services in 1968. It was one of the last Fodens to be fitted with the S21 cab, seen here in an insulated, double roof, version. The 6X6/22 model was powered by a Gardner 6LX-150 engine and is seen prior to export at Elworth Works in Sandbach. *(Author's collection)*

Right: Hong Kong-based Green Island Cement Co. took delivery of this 6AXB6/40 double drive tractor unit in 1967. It pulls a frameless BTC semi-trailer fitted with an Interconsult 750 bulk tank equipped with an Atco compressor, which was driven by a Volkswagen 1200 industrial engine. The Gardner 6LXB-180-powered tractor unit was fitted with the export version of the rigid S36 cab, the S37. This tractor unit was also used for pulling logging pole trailers, hence the sturdy "headache" rack fitted behind the vehicle's cab. *(David Bloor collection)*

Right: The Lion Rock Tunnel of Hong Kong took delivery of this remarkable piece of equipment in 1977. It was based on an AG18/30 model S83-cabbed tractor unit, which was powered by a modest, but very reliable Gardner 6LXB-180 engine. It had Swedish-built EKA recovery equipment fitted, which consisted of a 34-tonne main winch, 5-tonne front winch, a 7-tonne underlift for suspended tows and two ground anchors. *(Fodens Ltd)*

converted into a compact recovery vehicle to keep the very busy tunnel free of broken down vehicles. It was fitted with Swedish-built EKA recovery equipment, which was capable of pulling 34 tonnes on its single line main winch. The S83-cabbed vehicle also had a 5-tonne single pull front winch and a 7-tonne underlift, which could tow a loaded 60-tonne g.c.w. combination. A modestly rated Gardner 6LXB-180 engine powered this specialist vehicle.

Philippines

Foden supplied Philippine companies with tipper and concrete mixer chassis in the 1960s. Concrete Aggregates Inc. took delivery of several tipper chassis fitted with S21 overseas type cabs in 1963. The FE6/20 vehicles were fitted with Foden FD6 Mark 6 engines, which produced 175bhp, and coupled to Foden twelve-speed gearboxes. The tipper was fitted with an 11 cubic yard steel tipping body and Pilot tipping gear. The concrete mixers had Ransomes & Rapier 6 cubic yard mixer drums.

Four years later this company operated seven FE6/20 tippers for hauling aggregates from the quarry, which was about 25 miles from Manilla. Most of them had Neville 14.5-cubic yard capacity, alloy tipping bodies fitted, which were raised and lowered by Edbro F47 twin hydraulic rams.

A subsidiary company, Inter Island Construction Co., operated a FETU6/24 two-axle tractor unit and a FE6/14 flatbed truck.

Left: One of two concrete mixer chassis delivered to Concrete Aggregates Inc. in Manila in the Philippines. It is a FE6/20 model, powered by a Foden FD6 Mark 6 engine, developing 175bhp. It had a Foden twelve-speed underdrive gearbox and was fitted with an overseas pattern S21 fibreglass cab. The 6 cubic yard concrete mixer was hydraulically driven, and was manufactured by Ransomes & Rapier. *(David Bloor collection)*

CHAPTER FIVE

Exports Australia and Pacific

Australia

Steamers

Foden steam traction engines and steam wagons were very popular Down Under during the 1900–35 period. The first 7 and 8hp compound traction engines were shipped to Australia in 1902. Foden's agent, Langwill Bros & Davies based in Melbourne, imported the first traction engines. They were used in conjunction with drawbar trailers for agricultural work but also for transporting goods and even for the movement of complete wooden houses and sheds. Langwill Bros imported well over 100 traction engines between 1902 and 1914. Another four were shipped directly to Hobart in Tasmania between 1905 and 1910. Some of the 7hp models were converted into showman's engines.

Five- and 6-ton steam wagons of the Colonial type were exported to Australia in the next decade, followed by many C-types in the 1920s and 1930s. The Australian

Bottom: This very old photograph shows a 1907 Foden 3SP sprung compound steamer pulling an early wooden drawbar pole trailer, which is loaded with a part of a huge trunk. The men in front of the impressive outfit are Albert (left) and Paddy (right) Griffith, who were dealers in second-hand steam engines. They were also nephews of the famous Australian bush ranger, Ned Kelly. *(John Sanderson collection)*

Blue Metal Co. operated C-type steam wagons in tipper form. Sawmills used them as logging vehicles to winch heavy trunks out of the forests.

A small number of Foden steamers have been restored by the Australians and are rallied regularly by their proud owners. They include a few 7hp traction engines, a showman's engine and some C types.

First Diesels

During the 1930s Foden was represented in Australia by Rasch Motors Pty Ltd, which was based in Waymouth Street, Adelaide. There was also a depot in Spencer Street, Melbourne. Rasch was also the agent for Federal trucks and Nash cars, which were manufactured in the USA. At the same time, Webster & Sons, based in Hobart, were appointed Foden agents for Tasmania on behalf of Rasch Motors.

Early R-type models, fitted with square Foden W2 coach-built cabs, were exported to Australia in 1934. They were soon followed by S9-cabbed DG models fitted with exposed radiators. Some were sold to Tasmania-based companies, including a heavy 6×4 tractor unit in 1937. This vehicle was originally fitted with Gardner 5LW engine but as it pulled a 20-ton payload tipping trailer, a Gardner 6LW soon replaced

this engine. Bryden & Peters (Sydney) manufactured the tipper, which was fitted with a front-end, single-ram telescopic hoist. It was still operated in the 1950s.

The Australian Blue Metal Co. (ABM) of Sydney operated quite a lot of DG-series Fodens fitted with the S10 cab. These vehicles hauled aggregates, but also timber and other building materials. Most of them were four-axle DG6/15 rigid eight tippers. Many of them were still working in the late 1960s and each one had clocked up well over 1.5 million miles by then. When the vehicles were no longer suitable for doing roadwork, they were converted into dump trucks to get an extended lease of life in one of ABM's quarries.

Above: Another Australian Blue Metal DG-series Foden, one of four purchased in 1948. The little DG6/7.5 tipper is seen at St Marys Quarries, New South Wales, loaded with gravel. It was powered by a Gardner 6LW engine, producing 102bhp. *(Author's collection)*

Left: The Australian Blue Metal Co. (ABM) of Sydney operated many DG-series Fodens in two-, three- and four-axle configurations. Some pulled drawbar trailers to increase payload, such as fleet number 72, a wartime Gardner 6LW-102-powered DG6/10 model, which is seen here. It was imported by ABM directly from Ceylon. After a long and hard life most DG-series were converted into dump truck tippers and continued off-road work in one of ABM's quarries for twenty-five to thirty years. *(Douglass Baglin/Tony Petch collection)*

Above: A post-war DGTU6/20 tractor unit operated by W.J. Cockerell of Pascoe Vale, Melbourne. The vehicle was named *Miss Waveley* and was loaded with two guillotines weighing 12 tons each. *(Douglass Baglin/supplied by Tony Petch)*

Diesel Motors

The Diesel Motor Co. (later Diesel Motors Pty. Ltd) became Foden's main agent after World War II. The company was founded by J.J. O'Neill, but his seven sons did all the hard work and were all on the board.

The managing director was Les O'Neill, who was also a director of the Australian Blue Metal Co. (ABM). Diesel Motors and ABM had their joint head offices in Sydney and had depots in Perth and Melbourne, and later also in Alice Springs.

Another depot, operated by Rasch Motors, was

Above: A post-war DG series, specifically a DG6/15 rigid eight, fully loaded with bagged cement. Fleet number 11 was operated by Roberts Bros, based in Cabramatta, New South Wales. It was powered by a Gardner 6LW engine, which produced 102bhp. *(John Sanderson collection)*

in Adelaide; when taken over by the O'Neill Bros in around 1951 it traded under the Diesel Company name. The Melbourne depot was called Diesel Services Pty. Ltd. Underhill, Day & Co. Pty. Ltd was another Foden agent with its premises in Brisbane. Finally, A.G. Webster & Sons of Hobart still operated as Foden's agent in Tasmania.

All Diesel Motors companies represented Fodens throughout the 1950s and 1960s. Towards the end of the 1950s, Diesel Motors' head offices moved from

Sydney to Auburn, New South Wales. The Australian Foden network was extended in the 1950s with Diesel Motors depots established in Cairns, Darwin and Broken Hill. Lambton Diesel Service Co. was appointed Foden Agent in Lambton. At the end of the 1950s, Diesel Motors had sold nearly 1,000 Fodens to operators all over the country. The company also represented Gardner and Swedish-built Bolinder and Penta diesel engines, Crane trailers and Pilot hydraulic tipping gear.

Post-War S18s

Many S18-cabbed Fodens found their way to Australia in the late 1940s and 1950s. Companies specialising in the construction, mining and heavy haulage industry operated quite a lot of them. In addition, many companies in central Australia used them for general haulage and moving livestock by operating the Fodens as road trains, many times pulling two or three drawbar trailers. Australian dairies also used Fodens in tractor–trailer and in rigid eight configurations. Sunny West Milk, based in Perth, even operated a four-axle FG8/24 tractor unit, powered by a Gardner 8LW-150 engine and pulling a 4,500-gallon tank trailer. The long wheelbase tractor unit also had a small tank body fitted just behind the cab. The dromedary-type outfit was run seven days a week and had completed 500,000 miles in just over five years when it was superseded by a new and similar S20-cabbed 5,100-gallon combination in 1963. In the early 1960s Gascoyne Trading of Carnarvon operated fourteen Foden vehicles; most of them were S18-cabbed tractor units. They transported fresh produce, like fruit and vegetables, from farms to market places in Western Australia. The daily fruit and vegetable service from Carnarvon to Perth involved a 700-mile non-stop trip that was completed in twenty-two hours by two drivers.

Above right: One of the early (c.1949) FG-series Fodens that hit the road in Australia was this nice FG5/7.5 model tipper. Fleet number D4 was powered by a frugal Gardner 5LW engine, which produced 85bhp. It was operated by Mayne Nickless Ltd, founded in 1868 by John Mayne and Enoch Nickless, who started a parcel service. In the 20th century the company provided freight services to all Australian cities and ports and in 1980 it became a specialist in providing healthcare and contract logistics. The company was eventually taken over by Symbion Health Ltd in 2005. *(Author's collection)*

Right: Amalgamated Collieries took delivery of these two Fodens, a FG6/15 and a FG6/12, in the early 1950s. Fleet number 6 and 4 were both powered by Gardner 6LW engines, which produced 112bhp. Both tippers were fitted with insulated, double roof, S18 cabs. The vehicles were based at Collie, a village about 125 miles south of Perth in Western Australia. *(John Sanderson collection)*

Above: Travancore Dairy was based in Kent Street, Ascot Vale in Victoria. It produced 90,000 bottles of milk a day in the early 1950s. To transport milk in bulk it operated this FGTU6/20 tractor unit and single axle semi-trailer, which dates from around 1951. It was powered by a Gardner 6LW engine, producing 112bhp. *(Tony Petch)*

Left: The Diesel Motor Co. from Sydney advertised Foden trucks in Australian truck magazines quite regularly. Here they recommend S18 tractor units for livestock haulage under the slogan: "Fast stock haulage at low cost". The advertisement dates from 1951 and was published in *Truck & Bus Transportation* magazine. *(Author's collection)*

Bottom: This Foden FG6/15 model carries an Australian-built Harman excavator. A Gardner 6LW powered the short wheelbase Foden eight-wheeler. It had a reinforced chassis to withstand the heavy crane. The S18 Mark 1 cab features a well in its roof to accommodate the crane's main boom and bucket jib. It is one of a small batch built for the New South Wales Railways Department in the early 1950s. *(Author's collection)*

One of N.S.W. Railways Department's Mobile Excavators built
by Harman on a Foden 6-cylinder 15-ton chassis.

Left: John Peterson operated this FGTU8/40 tractor unit, here pulling a single axle semi-trailer, which is nicely sheeted for the trip. It is striking that the tractor unit is fitted with an additional load space above its cab, which is supported by steel bars secured to the front bumper and behind the cab. The tractor unit dates from around 1956 and was powered by a Gardner 8LW-150 straight eight engine. It was mostly used on the Sydney–Cairns route. *(Tony Petch collection).*

Opposite: Warwick Bryce's 1955 FGTU8/40 is occasionally still hard at work in the Melbourne area, as this picture shows. It features 1950s engineering coupled to modern modular platform trailer technology! Powered by an eight-cylinder Gardner, it has only 150bhp available, so it probably does the job a little slower than modern tractor units. The outfit is moving the upper part of an old excavator. *(Author's collection)*

Right: Foden exported some very heavy tractor units to Australia in the 1950s. This FGTU8/80 tractor unit is pulling a low-loader that carries a heavy Hackbridge transformer. The outfit is reversing into an electric power plant and is being watched by many people. The photograph was taken in Sydney's Darling Harbour area, which was a former dockside. It was transformed into a prestigious recreation area in the 1980s. *(Author's collection)*

All available axle configurations could be seen in most parts of Australia. The Foden sales programme started with the smaller FG 4×2 rigid chassis, followed by the heavier FG six- and eight-wheelers. FGTU tractor units were shipped to Australia in 4×2, 6×4 and even in 8×4 configurations. Until 1950 Gardner engines powered all Foden lorries, but from 1951 onwards Foden's own two-stroke engines also became available.

The biggest Foden customer in Australia was the Australian Blue Metal Co. which operated more than sixty vehicles in 1956, most of them being four-axle FG6/15 and FG6/24 models. Some of them were involved in the resealing of a 1,000-mile stretch of the Stuart Highway between Alice Springs and Darwin. ABM used a mobile crushing and screening plant, which was mounted on ex-US Army Rogers tank transporter trailers. Two four-axle FG8/15 model Fodens, fitted with S18 cabs and Gardner 8LW-150 engines, pulled two of these drawbar trailers. Each trailer weighed 45 tons, which resulted in gross combination weights of well over 100 tons. When the slow, but sturdy Fodens, had to negotiate short, steep hills they had to uncouple the second trailer and take the first to the top of each gradient. Then they had to collect the second one and recouple it to the first one at the top of the hill, which was a time consuming affair.

Foden Buses

During the 1940s and 1950s, more than forty bus and coach chassis were exported to Australia. Apart from the specially designed chassis, Foden also produced several standard FG-type goods vehicle chassis, which were converted into passenger vehicles. Finally, Foden also sold S18-cabbed FGTU tractor units to Australian companies, which pulled passenger-carrying semi-trailers.

The first single deck bus chassis, a Gardner 6LW-powered PVSC6 model, was sent to Australia in 1947. It was used as a demonstrator for about four years and was finally sold to a Tasmanian operator in 1951. Modern Transport and Metal Industries bodied it with a thirty-one-seat and goods compartment body. This chassis was soon followed by a couple of single deck PVSC6 chassis, which were fitted with double deck bodies by

the Australian Commonwealth Engineering Co. They were destined for the Punchbowl Bus Company of Riverwood, Sydney, and gave good service until around 1960. The double deck bodies were removed then and both vehicles were rebodied as single deck buses and worked for another ten years before taken out of service in 1970.

Diesel Motors of Sydney exhibited a PVSC6 chassis during the 1950 Sydney Easter Show. In the same year the Western Australian Government Railway (WAGR) purchased no fewer than twenty PVSC6 chassis, which were bodied by the Commonwealth Engineering Co.. The company took delivery of its first PVSC6 bus chassis and four FGTU tractor units for railway passenger road services in 1948. The semi-trailers accommodated sixty-two seated passengers and during rush hours numerous standing passengers increased the vehicles' capacity. Some of the 1950s buses, which had all metal bodies, had full seating for thirty-eight passengers, while others had eighteen seats and additional cargo compartments. Most export buses had a 21ft wheelbase, while the

Above: The Western Australian Government Railways operated standard Foden tractor units in combination with passenger carrying semi-trailers. This is a Gardner 6LW-powered FGTU6/20 model from the early 1950s. The semi-trailer could accommodate sixty-two seated passengers plus a fairly big number of standing passengers. This photograph shows that no bus stop signs were necessary in order to pick up passengers in remote areas in Western Australia. *(Peter Tulloch collection).*

home market vehicles had 16ft 6in, 17ft 6in or 19ft 6in wheelbases. Many of these WAGR vehicles clocked up more than a million miles and the last ones were put out of service as late as 1975, which says more than enough about the reliability and longevity of the Foden chassis and the Commonwealth bodies.

Although Diesel Motors offered the new rear-engined Foden bus chassis from 1950 onwards, most operators preferred the front-engine chassis. Only five rear-engine PVRG6 buses were sold in Australia, all fitted with Gardner 6LW engines and Motor Body Assemblers (Sydney) bodies. One of them was sold to

Left: Australia was Foden's biggest market for bus and coach chassis outside Great Britain. In all, forty-three chassis were exported to this country. Around twenty of these were operated by the Western Australia Government Railways. This 1950 PVSC6 bus chassis carried a locally built Commonwealth Engineering body, which seated eighteen passengers. The body also provided a large goods compartment. It was powered by a Gardner 6LW engine. *(Peter Tulloch collection)*

Right: Hampton Red Bus Services operated several second-hand Foden buses and coaches, including two of the famous observation coaches (called "camelbacks" in Australia). However, UV811 was purchased new in 1950. This PVSC6 model was originally fitted with a Symons & Fowler thirty-eight-seat body. A new Cheetham & Borwick body was fitted in 1963, seating thirty-nine passengers. The vehicle was re-registered HLC128 and was put out of service in the 1970s, after more than twenty years of service. *(Peter Tulloch collection)*

Rutty's Bus Service of Wollongong in 1952. Three other chassis went into service in 1953 and 1954 with the Cogee–Spearwood Bus Service, based in Perth. The two-stroke Foden FD6 Mark 1 and 2 engines were not available for the Australian bus market.

A remarkable passenger vehicle was Len Tuit's FG6/7.5 goods chassis fitted with a bus body. The 33ft long vehicle also pulled a two-axle drawbar trailer for carrying Royal Mail letters and parcels. It provided a weekly trunk service between Darwin and Alice Springs in the Northern Territory, a distance of 960 miles. It also maintained a regular bus service to Mount Isa.

Above: This stunning vehicle was one of the very few Foden buses that served in the Northern Territories. The 1956-built FG6/7.5 model was a normal truck chassis, which was fitted with a 33ft-long Motor Body Assemblers body, seating forty passengers. It pulled a 33ft drawbar trailer fitted with an enclosed body to carry post for Royal Mail. Len Tuit operated a weekly passenger and mail service between Alice Springs and Darwin, a round trip of almost 2,000 miles. *(Peter Tulloch collection)*

Successful S20s and S21s

The new Foden HG-series was a special export version, fitted with the timber-framed and aluminium- or steel-panelled S20 cab. The first chassis arrived in Australia in 1959 and were braked by a full air system and equipped with power steering. They were very popular in three- and four-axle prime mover form (HG6/20 and HG6/24). One of the first companies that took delivery of two HG6/20 chassis was Universal Concrete. Gardner 6LX-150 engines powered these concrete mixers, which had Howard donkey engines fitted to power the 6.5 cubic yard mixers. The cabs had special double tropical roofs fitted to keep out the heat as much as possible.

Heavy duty 6×4 prime movers could be fitted with Gardner 6LX and 8LW-engines (HG models), which both produced 150bhp or Cummins NH220 engines (HC model). The Foden FD6 Mark 6 two-stroke engine, which produced 175bhp (HE model), and Rolls–Royce engines (HR model) were also an option. Long distance tractor units and rigids were regularly fitted with narrow "bolt-on" sleeper cabs, which were called doghouses by many drivers. Later, full sleeper cab

Above right: Rigid eight-wheelers could easily be converted into heavy tractor units if work demanded. KWK Transport of Wyndham used several of these tractor units and flatbed trailers to deliver steel constructions for the Old River diversion dam in the north-western part of Australia. Fleet number 5 dates from around 1960 and had a Cummins NH220 engine. The S20 cab features a double roof and sleeper cab extension, which was often called the "doghouse". *(Author's collection)*

Right: Ron Thompson Haulage, based in South Grafton, New South Wales, operated this FCTU6/40 tractor unit, which dates from 1962. The 60-ton gross weight combination pulls an Australian-built Freighter low-loader that carries two Caterpillar Traxcavator 933s. The S20 cab has a sleeper extension and double roof. The outfit was operated between Alice Springs and Darwin. The Cummins NH220-powered vehicle was equipped with a heavy steel bumper and bull bar fitted underneath to avoid damage inflicted by kangaroos, which were encountered regularly on these trips. Note the typical 1960s Australian hand indicator just below the big shiny mirror. *(Niels Jansen collection)*

Left: Gascoyne Trading of Carnarvon became a very loyal Foden customer from the 1950s onwards. This FCTU6/40 model was fitted with a S20 cab featuring a double roof, sleeper cab extension, protective equipment to reduce damage in case of animal collisions and an additional searchlight just below the cab's double roof. The 1961 Cummins NH220-powered tractor unit pulls a semi-trailer, which has a corrugated body and sheeted open top. *(Niels Jansen collection)*

Right: The HG-series was specially designed for the Australian market. This HGTU6/30 model has a Gardner 6LX-150 engine fitted, coupled to a Foden twelve-speed gearbox. It was built in 1962 and operated by the South Coast Equipment Co., which was based in Unanderra, New South Wales. The tractor unit was fitted with a double roof, steel export S20 cab. Note the twin fire extinguishers stored behind the front bumper bar and the transversely fitted fuel tank behind the cab, which were early safety measures for fuel tankers. *(Author's collection)*

FODEN EXPORT VEHICLES

Right: A S20-cabbed 8×4 concrete mixer, which dates from the early 1960s. It was operated by the well-known Readymix concrete company that operated concrete plants in many parts of the world, including Great Britain, Germany, Austria, Italy, Israel and Trinidad. This vehicle was supplied by Foden agent Diesel Motors in Perth, Western Australia. It has had its headlamps moved from the cab's front panel to a special heavy bumper bar. Also note the hand-operated indicator sign mounted on the driver's door. *(John Sanderson collection)*

Right: To raise payload, quite a few Foden eight-wheelers were converted into ten-wheelers by adding an additional fifth, non-driven, axle. A good example is this HG6/24 model from around 1962, which was seen at a scrapyard waiting for a load. The S20 cab is equipped with windscreen protection and a heavy steel bumper bar. A modestly rated Gardner 6LX-150 engine powered this heavy truck, which could easily reach a gross weight of 35 to 40 tons. *(Author's collection)*

Left: An early 1960s Foden fitted with a S20 sleeper cab conversion in the Northern Territory in 1981. After twenty years of service the two-stroke powered Foden was still going strong with a well drilling company. Its nine-speed gearbox could only take it to a top speed of 30mph. Note the heavy bull bar with the steel chains draped around it. *(Rufus Carr)*

Opposite: A very long wheelbase Foden HG tractor unit in sunny New South Wales in the early 1960s. The tractor unit features an upright exhaust system, S20 cab fitted with a sturdy front bumper, typical shiny Australian mirror set-up and double air horns on the roof. The Gardner 6LX-150-powered tractor unit was operated by Canberra Washed Sand Pty and pulled a two-axle tipping semi-trailer. *(Niels Jansen collection)*

Left: Many Fodens were operated in the logging industry, like this early 1960s, long wheelbase HG 6×4 tractor unit. It has no mudguards over its rear bogie and there is enough room on the chassis to bolt on a spare wheel and a large fuel tank just behind the cab. It certainly gives ample ground clearance for off-road work. The long pole trailer carries a variety of cut down trees, which have been chained down neatly. *(Niels Jansen collection)*

Left: South Australian Barytes Ltd operated this HGTU6/40 model between its mine at Flinders and the railhead at Hawker. The Gardner 6LX-150-powered vehicle was put into service in 1962, annually delivering 12,000 tons of baryte minerals, containing barium sulphate. The 20 cubic yard semi-trailer was manufactured by the Superlift Equipment Co. but had a four-sprung Foden bogie. The tractor unit was fitted with the export version of the S20 cab and an enlarged radiator to provide additional cooling in hot weather. *(John Sanderson collection)*

Right: An S21-cabbed Foden tipper is leaving a weighbridge with a Volvo F7 eight-wheeler waiting for its turn. This nice looking vehicle was more than twenty years old when this photograph was taken. The 1962, Gardner 6LX-150-powered, FG6/24 model was operated by John. L. Pierce.
(Author's collection)

Right: Aboods Transport of Ermington, New South Wales, was a major Foden operator. Fleet number 28 dates from around 1963 and pulls a wide-spread axle flatbed semi-trailer loaded with cable reels. The S21 fibreglass cab was fitted with an add-on sleeper cab. *(John Sanderson collection)*

Left: Jamiesons of Bunbury, a town south of Perth in Western Australia, operated this impressive 1965 tipper combination. The 8AX6/24 model is an adapted rigid eight-wheeler that operated as a tractor unit. Porters of Perth built the 27 cubic yard tipper trailer, which was fitted with an Edbro 30-ton single hydraulic ram. The outfit hauled ilmenite from an opencast mine at Capel to Bunbury, from where it was shipped to places all over the world. *(Niels Jansen collection)*

Left: This beautiful color photograph was taken around 1967. It shows a 6AXB6/40 model tractor unit fitted with a fibreglass S21 cab featuring a sleeper extension and double roof. A Gardner 6LXB-180 powers this 6×4 tractor unit, which pulls a Freighter semi-trailer fitted with a Transicold Freezer installation. Gascoyne Trading used this combination for transporting fresh produce between Exmouth, Carnarvon and Port Hedland in Western Australia. *(Niels Jansen collection)*

Opposite: All 150 horse power of the Gardner 6LX engine were needed to climb out of the Griffin opencast coal mine near Collie in Western Australia. The 8X6/28 chassis was fitted with a S21 cab and home-made 23 cubic yard tipper body, which had Edbro front end tipping gear. The vehicle transported coal to the MUJA power station, only half a mile down the road. *(David Bloor collection)*

Right: Bell Bros Pty Ltd was an earth moving and road building contractor based in Guildford, Western Australia. It operated this impressive S21-cabbed 8×4 tractor unit, which is pulling a two-axle tipping semi-trailer. The tractor unit dates from the early 1960s and was photographed by John Rae in 1967 when working on a contract with A.V. Jennings to build the township of Dampier. It also features a typical Australian chromed mirror set-up, which is quite similar to the set-ups used in the USA. A couple of years later Bell Bros became an importer of ERF trucks. *(John Sanderson collection)*

EXPORTS AUSTRALIA AND PACIFIC ————

conversions became available, as Foden did not offer a factory-fitted sleeper cab on the S20s. Foden shipped the vehicles in completely knocked down form. Diesel Motors assembled the S20 type Fodens in its facilities at Auburn, some 12 miles from Sydney. After assembling they were sent to all parts of Australia, such as the tropical Northern Territory, Western Australia and New South Wales. Many of the New South Wales-based Foden operators used their vehicles for livestock transport, particularly sheep.

Most Australian operators were not keen on plastic cabs and that is why many preferred the S20. Nevertheless, vehicles fitted with the fibreglass S21 cabs were sold to Australian operators in the 1960s, particularly after the production of S20 cabs ceased in 1964. Gascoyne Trading was one of the operators that took delivery of several Gardner 6LX-150-powered, 6AX6/40 model double drive tractor units fitted with S21 cabs. Sunny West dairies put some more giant dromedary milk tankers into service, which also had S21 cabs fitted. The load capacity was increased to 5,200 gallons of milk and the gross combination weight to 41 tons. Similar four-axle, S21-cabbed, 8AX6/24 tractor units were operated in the construction industry in conjunction with large tipping semi-trailers. The tractor units were, in fact, modified rigid eights fitted with fifth wheels to couple up to semi-trailers. They were also widely used in the logging industry. S21 cabs were normally fitted with double-skin roofs and sleeper cab extensions were favoured by many long distance hauliers.

North Australian Haulage (NAH) bought its first Foden in 1960 and soon became the dealer for the Darwin/Katherine area in north Australia. It operated some tippers in 10×4 configuration, which were fitted with S21 cabs and heavy bull bars to protect the fibreglass cabs. The 8C6/24 model vehicles were powered by Cummins NH220 engines and had Franklyn air suspension on the fifth axle.

Northern Territory Road Trains

Before World War II it was not easy to transport goods to the remote and sparsely populated parts of Australia. There were not many railway tracks in places such as Western Australia, the Northern

Territory and Queensland either, so most freight had to be transported by truck. The federal government had plans to construct a railway connection from Darwin in the north to Alice Springs, but these plans did not materialise until 2004, when a 1,559km long railway track was opened between both cities. From 2 February 2004, passenger and freight trains used this new railway connection, which eventually ended in Adelaide, 2,979km from Darwin. The Ghan (or Afghan Express) passenger line now leaves Darwin and Adelaide once or twice a week for a two-day journey to the other side of the country.

Lots of goods, such as livestock, fuel and mining products, needed to be transported in large quantities or in bulk. However, as load capacities of trucks were not very high at the time, hauliers and the Australian government looked for higher capacity vehicles. This resulted in an experiment that was begun by the Australian government when it ordered a special designed road train, which was built by the British AEC company. The first road train entered Australia in 1934 and consisted of an eight-wheel prime mover, which had all-wheel drive and two steering axles, one

Above: A 1952 Foden road train fitted with livestock bodies on truck and two drawbar trailers. It could move 500 sheep per trip at a speed of 18mph. The Foden FG8/15 is one of the first export vehicles equipped with an 8LW Gardner in-line engine, which produced 150bhp. It was operated by J. Allison, based in Broken Hill, New South Wales. *(John Sanderson collection)*

at the front and the other located at the back of the vehicle. It pulled two purpose-built Dyson four-axle drawbar trailers, which followed the prime mover's track. The whole combination measured nearly 72ft (about 22m) and had a load capacity of 15 tons, 3 on the prime mover's back and 6 tons on each trailer. An AEC 8.8-litre diesel engine, producing 130bhp, powered this impressive outfit. A four-speed gearbox and three-speed auxiliary box provided twelve gears. The "government road train", as it became appropriately known, was put into service in the Northern Territory, operating from Alice Springs. A journey to Tennant Creek took about twenty-three hours and top speed was less than 30mph. This was quite an achievement, bearing in mind that there were no roads, but only dirt tracks at the time.

The AEC road train was operated for twelve years, covering around 850,000 miles in total. This vehicle laid the foundations for the future development of the Australian road trains.

Constructing the famous Stuart Highway in 1942 enhanced the development of the Northern Territory enormously. The 1,000-mile road connected Darwin with Alice Springs, which had a railhead, connecting the town with Adelaide in the southern part of the country. The sealed highway was built by an American–Australian consortium and was vital for the southward movement of war supplies, which were shipped to Darwin. A second road, called the Barkly Highway, was constructed between Alice Springs and Mount Isa in Queensland.

After World War II these highways were widely used by transport companies to move all sorts of commodities, livestock and bulk goods to all parts of Australia. American Diamond Ts and Federals soon became the backbone of the Australian road trains. Pioneers including Kurt Johannsen and Dave Baldock operated road trains that pulled up to seven trailers! They moved at modest speeds of between 20 and 25 miles an hour without having brakes on the trailers, so controlling a nearly 190ft (57m) long combination weighing more than 100 tons was not an easy job.

Many British-built vehicles replaced these American vehicles when the Australian government introduced legislation on size and weights of road trains in 1954. Although extremely long road trains were still allowed for economical reasons during some years, most were restricted to pull three trailers. New laws were introduced in 1961 restricting axle weights to 8.5 tons for single axles and 16 tons for the double drive bogies. This allowed three-axle prime movers pulling two four-axle trailers or three smaller trailers at gross weights up to 88 tons. The 1954 legislation created big opportunities for Foden vehicles as they had strong chassis and were fitted with low revving Gardner engines, which produced enough torque to pull several trailers. Foden road trains were soon operated in the Northern Territory and Queensland. Fodens were initially fitted with the very reliable and frugal Gardner 6LW engine, which produced 112bhp, a little later followed by the big Gardner 8LW engine, which was a straight eight lump that offered 150bhp.

In 1950 a co-ordinated road–rail service was set up by a number of independent hauliers, who operated from the railhead of Alice Springs. The service was simply called Co-ord Service and moved goods between Alice Springs, Larrimah and Darwin. It was formed to provide a fast and cheap service to the northern part of the country but it took until 1953 before it was in full operation. In 1956 the service was extended east to Mount Isa. Well-known Australian hauliers such as Dave Baldock, the Kittle Bros, Stan Cawood, Allan C. Allwright and Ted Stiles (Outback Transport) soon operated one or more Gardner-powered Fodens fitted with S18 cabs. Some operated 6×4 or 8×4 rigids, while others chose 4×2 or 6×4 tractor units, but almost all vehicles pulled additional trailers. In 1957 Co-ord Service went into container haulage by introducing the Rudder's Cargotainer Service. Heavy overhead gantry cranes at the railhead in Alice Springs loaded the containers on to the cargo decks of the trucks and trailers. The Co-ord Service members operated many Foden road trains during the

Right: Wright Carriers based in Mount Isa operated this 1962 Foden road train in the Northern Territory hauling a variety of goods. Normally this outfit would move livestock, an activity that is painted on the doors, but it also moved road construction equipment including these wheeled road graders. It is fitted with a S20 cab that features a double skin roof and a sleeper cab extension. The model HR6/20 is powered by a 210bhp Rolls–Royce C6N engine and covered more than 100,000 miles a year. *(David Bloor collection)*

Opposite: Peninsula Freighters operated this cattle train in Queensland and the Northern Territories in the 1960s. The prime mover pulls two drawbar trailers fitted with simple, half-open, livestock bodies. The vehicle is photographed at high speed travelling over dusty outback roads. The Cummins NH220 engine is coupled to a Foden twelve-speed gearbox to make good progress. *(John Sanderson collection)*

Left: Allwright Transport was one of the Co-ord members that ran Foden road trains. It operated from Alice Springs with this early 1960s HC6/24 model, which was powered by a Cummins NH220 engine and fitted with the export version of the S20 cab that also had a bolt-on sleeper compartment. Fleet number 8 was christened *The Wheel of Fortune* and had a load of 78 tons of copper ore on the truck and three drawbar trailers. Overall weight was a staggering 112 tons. *(David Bloor collection)*

booming 1950s and 1960s. The specially designed HG series, which were equipped with S20 double roof sleeper cabs, became extremely popular with road train operators. Fitted with Cummins NH220 engines, these vehicles could handle 100-ton gross weights, which made Foden "king of the road" in the Northern Territory in the early 1960s. Fodens moved cattle, machinery, fuel, containers, cars and all sorts of other commodities in large quantities from Darwin to Alice Springs and Mount Isa and vice versa day in, day out, clocking up to 2,500 miles a week.

At the end of the 1950s, American trucks fitted with very powerful engines entered the country. Mack, White, International and Kenworth trucks became quite popular from the early 1960s onwards and replaced many British-built vehicles. Foden answered the challenge by fitting Cummins and Rolls–Royce engines as an option, because Gardner could not keep up with the demand for high-powered units. Foden's own two-stroke engine, particularly the powerful 225bhp FD6 Mark 7 engine, was tried by some operators but was not a success in the harsh conditions vehicles operated in. Most operators definitely preferred Cummins engines, in particular the NH220. Thanks to these powerful engines Foden was still able to sell quite a few S20- and S21-cabbed vehicles during the 1960s. At the end of the 1960s, legislation allowed larger road trains. Rigid trucks could pull three trailers, but were restricted to 44m, while tractor–trailer combinations (triples) were allowed to measure 50m at 115-ton gross weights. The very stiff competition from American-built trucks was the main reason that Foden sales declined rapidly in the late 1960s. It also heralded the end of Foden road trains in Australia.

Dump Trucks

The first dump trucks that were exported to Australia had adapted S18 cabs fitted. Selmer Engineering bought a fleet of FGD6 dump trucks in the late 1940s and operated them for many years on a huge hydroelectric project in the Snowy Mountains in New South Wales. The Australian Blue Metal Co. also operated Foden dump trucks in its quarries, as did Davis Contractors of Sydney and the Cockburn Cement Co. in Western Australia.

Dump Truck Road Trains

A specially designed heavy dump truck fitted with a half cab was delivered to Peko Mines at Tennant Creek in the Northern Territory of Australia in 1967. It was a road train type three-axle tipper, which pulled two drawbar trailers. The prime mover and both four-axle trailers were fitted with tipper bodies, which could only tip sideways. Each body was fitted with a single 30-ton hydraulic ram that gave a tipping angle of 50 degrees.

The Foden 6C6/80 dump truck was powered by a Cummins NHK250 engine and mated to a Foden twelve-speed gearbox. The design was based on a heavy haulage tractor unit and adapted for dump truck work. It was designed for a gross weight of around 100 tons, which meant that a payload of 70 tons was possible. In reality the vehicle was loaded with 80 tons of ore regularly and achieved gross weights of up to 115 tons. The operators chose road transport because a rail connection was considered to be too expensive as relatively low volumes had to be shifted.

Below: This 1967 Foden 6C6/80 dump truck was powered by a Cummins NHK250 engine, mated to a Foden twelve-speed gearbox. It was designed for a gross weight of around 100 tons. In reality the vehicle was loaded with 80 tons of ore regularly and achieved gross weights of up to 115 tons. The impressive outfit hauled gold ore over a private road from mines in Ivanhoe and Orlando to the Peko mill at an average speed of 23mph. *(David Bloor collection)*

The vehicle had to haul gold ore over a private road from mines in Ivanhoe and Orlando to the Peko mill. Loading the vehicle was done from an overhead bin that was equipped with four chutes. Discharging the load was achieved by tipping sideways into a 400-ton capacity underground bin. The prime mover's tipper body had a capacity of 15 cubic yard and each trailer was fitted with bigger 20 cubic yard bodies. The overall length of the whole combination was 75ft. The dump truck was the second Foden prime mover to be added to the Peko fleet. The first one was a S21-cabbed, Cummins NH220-powered, FNCTU6/80 model, purchased in the early 1960s.

Plastic Cabs

The first Fodens fitted with the new fibreglass S24 tilt cab arrived in Australia in 1964. A TE6/30 tractor unit, powered by a Foden two-stroke engine, was one of the first S24-cabbed vehicles that was put into service. TE7/30 tractor units, which had 225bhp Foden FD6 Mark 7 engines fitted, soon followed them. The Australian Blue Metal Co., which was a subsidiary of Ready Mixed Concrete, still operated many Fodens at the time. Its fleet included 6AX6/40 double drive tractor–tipping semi-trailer combinations fitted with S24 tilt cabs and Gardner 6LX-150 engines.

Aboods Transport of North Mead, Sydney, was another big Foden operator, which regularly put new vehicles into service. In 1963 a model FETU6/30 tractor unit fitted with S21 sleeper cab and 175bhp Foden FD6 Mark 6 engine was added, while two years later a FGTU6/30 tractor unit fitted with S24 tilting sleeper cab and Gardner 6LX-150 engine joined the fleet.

Western Australia-based Master Dairy took delivery of a Foden S24-cabbed dromedary milk tanker combination in 1967. The 8×4 long wheelbase model 8X6/28 tractor unit had a Gardner 6LX-150 engine and a Foden twelve-speed gearbox. The milk tank, mounted on the prime mover, had a capacity of 1,500 gallons, while the semi-trailer's tank had two compartments of 2,000 gallons each. The 5,500-gallon combination did two daily trips between Wagerup and Perth, a distance of some 80 miles.

Foden set up a new sales organisation in July 1968. Fodens Ltd was now based in Moorebank, Liverpool, New South Wales. The Fodens shipped from Great Britain arrived in unit-kit form at Moorebank and Fodens Ltd adapted them to customers' requirements and also provided the servicing. Foden agents Diesel Motors still operated branches in Bentley, Brisbane and Adelaide.

The S24 tilt cab was superseded by the S34 in 1966, while a year later a fixed version was introduced. This was the S36 cab, which was much used in the construction industry and fitted to many tippers and concrete mixers. Both cabs consisted of fibreglass shells, floor and both doors, and they had double CAV headlamps fitted. These cabs were also exported to Australia, but had different designations (S35 and S37 respectively). They differed from the British cabs by having double-skinned roofs, integrated sun visors and by being 2.5in narrower. Fodens fitted with S35 tilt cabs were used by Aboods, which took delivery of a 6×4 tractor unit in 1968 that was powered by a Gardner 6LXB-180 and equipped

Below: One of the first Foden tractor units fitted with the new S24 glassfibre tilt cab was delivered to K.P. Neal of Melbourne in 1964. The TE6/30 model was powered by a Foden FD6 Mark 6 two-stroke engine, producing 175bhp, which was coupled to a Foden twelve-speed gearbox. The tractor unit pulls a frameless 6,000-gallon capacity tank trailer, which was made of aluminum. The vehicle was photographed outside the Diesel Motors depot in Melbourne. *(John Sanderson collection)*

Right: Australian Blue Metal operated this nice 6×4 tractor unit and 20 cubic yard capacity tipper trailer, which was manufactured by Geecham of Adelaide. The outfit is painted in the Ready Mixed Concrete and ABM livery, as they were sister companies. The tractor unit is a 6AX6/40 model, which means that it was a six-wheeler tractor unit. It had a Gardner 6LX-150 engine and a gross combination weight of 40 tons. *(David Bloor collection)*

Left: Masters Dairy operated this 8X6/28 tractor unit and milk semi-trailer between Wagerup and Perth in Western Australia twice a day. The tractor unit was fitted with a 1,500-gallon tank, while the semi-trailer contained two tanks of 2,000 gallons each. It was powered by a Gardner 6LX-150 engine coupled to a Foden twelve-speed underdrive gearbox. The 41-ton combination dates from 1967 and was fitted with a S24 tilt cab. It was photographed in front of the Diesel Motors premises in Bentley, which was also a Mercedes–Benz truck dealer. Master Dairy operated more of these Foden "dromedary" outfits fitted with S20 and S40 cabs. *(Author's collection)*

Left: Aboods Transport of Northmead (Sydney) could not foresee that Foden would become a part of the American Paccar company in 1980. Nevertheless it already operated a Kenworth-cabbed Foden tractor unit in the 1970s. This vehicle started life as a FRTU6/40 model in 1965 fitted with a S21 cab. Fleet number 49 was rebuilt later in its life by fitting a Rolls–Royce 340 engine, a Kenworth K100 cab, Fuller transmission, Hendrickson suspension and Eaton axles. This unusual vehicle is still owned by the Abood family in memory of founder Cedric Abood and displayed regularly at truck shows. Note the Atkinson front hubcaps. *(Author's collection)*

Left: A demonstrator tipper chassis, model 8XB6/28, fitted with the export version of the S36 rigid cab designated the S37. The "Cleanline" aluminium tipper body was fabricated by Highgate Engineers based in Rochdale, Queensland. The tipper chassis was powered by a Gardner 6LXB-180 engine. *(Tony Petch collection)*

with a sleeper cab extension. The rigid eight was also popular in brick carrier and tipper form.

A slightly bigger and updated fixed fibreglass cab was introduced in 1970. The S39 cab had double windscreens, while the S34 and S36 had single piece windscreens. The export version of the S39 was called the S38. In the early 1970s quite a few rigid eight tankers, model 8XB6/24 fitted with Gardner 6LXB-180 engines, were delivered to Caltex Oil, which had depots in Sydney and other major Australian cities. Other S38 rigid eights were operated by many Australian tipper companies, which fitted aluminium tipper bodies. This configuration also featured the popular Gardner 6LXB engine in most cases. S38-cabbed tractor units also found their way to Australia. An Australian operator, Mr Woolley of Lithgow, New South Wales, ordered a model 4AXB6/30 two-axle tractor unit in early 1970, which pulled a two-axle tipping trailer to transport coal from a colliery to power stations. His estate was appropriately called Elworth Park, the name of the Sandbach factory, as he operated another two three-axle Foden tippers, which originated from the mid-1950s and were still operated in the early 1970s.

Above right: Rochedale of Brisbane delivered texture bricks to building sites with this 1970 long wheelbase Foden 8XB6/24. The brick carrier was powered by a Gardner 6LXB-180 engine and fitted with an export S35 tilt cab. *(David Bloor collection).*

Right: Arthur Thomson and his wife emigrated from Scotland to Australia in 1962. Arthur soon became an owner-driver and purchased this Foden 4AXB6/30 tractor unit new in 1972. It was powered by a Gardner 6LXB-180 engine and fitted with the export version of the S36 fixed cab, designated S37, which is converted into a sleeper cab. Arthur had a contract with Wridgways Removals & Storage to transport furniture from Sydney to Brisbane and back again, a round trip of 1,260 miles. *(David Bloor collection)*

New Steel Cab

Prior to the introduction of Foden's new S40 steel cab at the Earls Court London Show in October 1968, Foden had directed severe trials in Australia to be sure that this new export cab could be operated under the harsh conditions found in many export countries. The company estimated no testing ground in the world would be more severe than the Australian outback, so a three-axle tractor unit powered by a Gardner 6LXB-180 engine appeared on the Australian dirt roads in spring 1968. The Motor Panels of Coventry-built

cab had a sleeper extension and was provided with a double-skin steel roof. The tests were executed in co-operation with Gascoyne Trading of Carnarvon in Western Australia, which provided a semi-trailer and two drivers. One of Foden's technical representatives and a service manager from Diesel Motors formed the test crew. The first part of the tests involved the 600-mile Carnarvon–Perth journey to the fruit markets and were pretty straightforward. Although the tractor unit had no Foden badges, the new vehicle was immediately recognised as a new model by quite a few Australian drivers. Showing the large chrome

Below: In spring 1968 a new Foden was seen in Western Australia. It was fitted with the steel S40 cab, which was manufactured by Motor Panels of Coventry and specially designed for export purposes. It was tested extensively in Australia to be sure it could operate under harsh conditions in remote areas. Dedicated Foden operator Gascoyne Trading of Carnarvon was chosen to test the new tractor unit, which was fitted with a factory-built sleeper cab. The 6AXB6/40 model had a Gardner 6LXB-180 engine fitted. *(Niels Jansen collection)*

Right: Mayne Nickless operated a number of these seven-axle drawbar combinations. This 8C6/28 model eight-wheeler was delivered in 1970 and powered by a Cummins NHK250 engine. The truck and drawbar trailer each carried two containers loaded with copper concentrate, which was transported from Kalgoorlie to railheads in Western Australia. The 55-ton combinations had steel S41 cabs. Diesel Motors Pty Ltd in Perth, which also had become Mercedes–Benz distributors at the time, supplied them. *(Niels Jansen collection)*

Left: Heavy duty 6×4 tractor unit in road train form, which was operated by the Ridolfo Group, now one of the largest transport companies in Western Australia. Italian immigrants Vince and Dominico Ridolfo started buying Fodens in the early 1960s. This 6AC6/75 model dates from 1972 and was powered by a Cummins NTK335 engine; ample power in those days for pulling an additional semi-trailer. *(Tony Petch collection)*

Left: Another eight-wheeler fitted with the steel Motor Panels cab. This vehicle had an S40 sleeper cab, which accommodated a Gardner 6LXB-180 engine. The 8XB6/32 model was operated by S. Amendola from Sydney and dates from April 1973. It had an additional steel roof plate fitted to keep some of the heat out of the cab. *(John Sanderson collection)*

Delta Cabs

American lightweight trucks became very popular in Australia in the early 1970s. UK-designed vehicles had higher tare weights in comparison with American designs and the front axles were set too far back. Australian weight regulations demanded vehicles with extremely wide wheelbases to comply with the existing legislation. Foden took up the challenge with the American competition. The Sydney-based Foden depot designed new chassis in conjunction with engineers from Foden UK. This resulted in a lightweight rigid

Above: As Foden wanted to compete with lightweight American trucks, the Sydney-based Foden depot designed a light chassis in co-operation with British company engineers. The chassis was fitted with a plastic cab built by Delta Marine of Melbourne. These vehicles became known as "Deltas". This 4AXB8/32 two-axle tractor unit had a Gardner 8LXB-240 engine fitted beneath its Delta sleeper cab. It was operated by Roy Pedemont Transport and is seen here brand new in 1973. *(Author's collection)*

Foden kite on the grille panel helped, of course. The next trip went in a northerly direction and ahead of Winning Pool a vast emptiness lay ahead. Despite some wiring problems, which caused a short circuit behind the dash panel, the test was continued. The outfit conquered heat, fords, floods, heavily corrugated roads and three tyre blow-outs before entering Port Hedland safely. The 555-mile journey had taken nearly twenty-five hours and the test crew was unanimous in their verdict: this new steel cab was "a real beaut". And they should know as they had driven it, ridden in it, slept in it and got underneath it under the most arduous conditions. A later version of this cab, which was much used in Australia, was the S41. This version had a deeper front grille panel to accommodate the larger Cummins 14-litre engines.

A long wheelbase Foden eight-wheeler was the star of the 1970 Adelaide Commercial vehicle show. The chassis was fitted with a S41 sleeper cab and powered by a Cummins NTK270 engine. S40/41-cabbed Fodens soon became popular in Australia in various configurations. Mayne Nickless copper mines near Kalgoorlie in Western Australia operated three-drawbar outfits equipped with four large containers. These vehicles were used to transport copper concentrate to railheads. The four-axle trucks, powered by Cummins NHK250 engines, pulled three-axle drawbar trailers and grossed 55 tons. Other S41-cabbed Fodens in the area were operated by the Capital Roads Department, based in Perth. The 6×4 day cab tractor units were involved with road construction jobs on main roads and motorways.

Right: One of the first Delta-cabbed Fodens to be assembled in Australia. The 8AXB6/32 model was delivered to Clark & Greenway of Bayswater, a suburb of Melbourne, in 1972. It was powered by a Gardner 6LXB-180 engine coupled to a Foden nine-speed gearbox. It was fitted with Eaton rear axles and Hendrickson walking beam rear suspension. The vehicle carried perishable goods from Sydney to Melbourne over a distance of 600 miles in around thirteen hours. *(John Sanderson collection)*

Opposite: Readymix Concrete Australia, which was a subsidiary of Foden distributor Diesel Motors Pty Ltd, operated this 1972 Delta-cabbed Foden tractor unit and tipper trailer. A huge Caterpillar 989 wheel loader dumps its load of aggregate in the tipper's body. It's obvious that tractor unit and semi-trailer formed a pair, as their fleet numbers were W2042 and W2043. The day cab tractor unit had a Gardner 8LXB-240 engine installed. *(Niels Jansen collection)*

Left: Aboods Transport of Northmead near Sydney also operated some Delta cab tractor units. This impressive 6AR6/40 model was fitted with a heavy bull bar, incorporating an additional, centrally fitted, searchlight. However, fleet number 56 started life as an early 1960s three-axle tractor unit fitted with an S20 cab. It was rebuilt in the early 1970s and fitted with a Delta cab and Rolls-Royce engine. *(Author's collection)*

eight chassis with maximum outer axle spread. The chassis was fitted with a sleeper cab, which could be tilted hydraulically, and was produced by Delta Marine of Melbourne. The vehicles were appropriately named "Deltas". Further specifications for the 8×4 rigid were a Gardner 6LXB-180 engine, Foden nine-speed gearbox, Eaton rear axles and a Hendrickson walking beam rear suspension. The next challenge was to design a range of heavy duty tractor units to regain a share of the road train market. These 6×4 tractor units were equipped with Gardner 8LXB-240 engines. As a result, two- and three-axle tractor units and four-axle rigids fitted with the Delta cab were manufactured in the 1972–75 period. Unfortunately they were only sold in small numbers; it is believed that twenty-six were manufactured. Loyal Foden operators including Aboods operated some Gardner and Rolls–Royce-powered Deltas. Ready

Mixed Concrete was another Delta operator, taking some 10×4 and 8×4 rigids and 6×4 tractors.

Bonneted Fodens

The Australian Foden assembly plant was transferred from Fodens Limited to the Diesel Motors branch in Bentley, near Perth, in 1972. Diesel Motors was now a subsidiary of the well-known Readymix Concrete Group. Sales and service in New South Wales was continued at Fodens Ltd in Moorebank near Sydney. The other Foden agents were still based in Adelaide, South Australia, and Brisbane, Queensland.

To provide a better ride characteristic, comfortable sleeping accommodation and air conditioning equipment, the Perth branch designed a bonneted 6×4 tractor unit for operations in Western Australia. Loyal

Foden operator Gascoyne Trading took delivery of two such innovative vehicles in 1972. One was powered by a Cummins NHC250 engine, which was coupled to a Foden twelve-speed gearbox and Foden two-spring rear axles. The other one had the more powerful Cummins NTC335 under its bonnet. A modified S40 cab was placed behind the imposing bonnet, which carried a

Below: Two of these imposing bonneted Fodens were delivered to Gascoyne Trading in 1972. The cab consisted of a steel S40 sleeper cab and a long additional bonnet to accommodate the big Cummins NTC335 engine. It provided better ride characteristics in comparison with the normal front cab layout. The two 6AC6/44 model vehicles were registered C4263 and C4264 and were operated by Gascoyne on regular runs between Geraldton and Carnarvon in West Australia. (*Niels Jansen collection*)

large Foden kite and Foden logo, while the front wings had double headlamps fitted. The cabs were equipped with air conditioning units. It is almost certain that only two of these tractor units were built.

Roberts Foden Fleet

Peter Roberts, born in Sydney in 1936, was a real Gardner man and stayed loyal to the famous British diesel engine marque during his whole life. In the early 1950s Peter became an apprentice with a commercial vehicle agent based in Sydney that maintained Gardner engines. After five years he joined his father Ross, who operated two Fodens fitted with Gardner engines at the time. The Fodens were kept busy with hauling sand and metal from the Emu Plains into the Sydney area. As the Foden fleet increased in the early 1960s Peter maintained his father's vehicles, but he also did some driving occasionally. He became his father's partner when his uncle pulled out of the business.

When Ross retired in 1971, Peter took over the company. Apart from carting sand, the company had acquired a profitable contract in the 1960s to transport Rocla concrete pipes. The Rocla plant, which was at Penrith, provided a lot of work for Peter Roberts' vehicles. During long periods in the late 1960s the company needed seven trucks a day during six days a week to complete a contract transporting pipe work

Above right: Peter Roberts operated ancient Foden vehicles well into the 1980s. He was a real Gardner man and stayed loyal to this marque during his whole life. He not only operated Fodens but also Gardner-powered ERFs and Atkinsons. This early 1950s FG6/12 model tipper was a good example of the durability of Foden vehicles. The photograph of the Gardner 6LW-powered vehicle was taken when the vehicle was nearly thirty years old. *(Author's collection)*

Right: A nice colour photograph featuring a FG6/24 model fitted with an S18 Mark 2 cab from around 1955, which was photographed by Judith Roberts. It was fitted with a heavy steel tipper body and powered by a Gardner 6LW engine, which had an output of 112bhp. *(Judith Roberts)*

Left: This striking display was set up in August 1965 at the Rocla Pipe Works during a demonstration for local council engineers. The S18 Mark 2-cabbed FGTU6/20 model dates from around 1950 and was powered by a Gardner 6LW engine. The double drive tractor unit and single axle semi-trailer were put on to specially prepared huge Rocla concrete pipes. *(Judith Roberts)*

Below left: This HGTU6/40 model tractor unit worked on contract for Rocla concrete pipes. The tractor unit had a S20 day cab fitted and was powered by a Gardner 6LX-150 engine. It was built in the early 1960s and seen parked up in the Roberts yard. *(Niels Jansen collection)*

Below: One of the most modern vehicles in Peter Roberts's fleet was this tipper that dates from 1972. It was fitted with a steel S41 cab and powered by a Gardner 8LXB engine. It was engaged on deliveries for the Blue Metal and Gravel quarrying company (BMG). The Roberts company was wound up in the late 1980s. *(Author's collection)*

to power stations in the Hunter Valley. Roberts' fleet consisted of many Foden S18-, S20- and S21-cabbed tractor units, but it also operated some ERF's and Atkinsons, all Gardner powered as a matter of course. The Rocla contract ended in the early 1980s, which resulted in concentrating on tipper work in the area. Peter Roberts operated the fine fleet of old Fodens well into the 1980s and some of them were engaged on deliveries for the Blue Metal and Gravel (BMG) quarrying company. At that time Roberts still operated S18-cabbed tippers; some of them had 10×4 configurations but most were 8×4 tipper chassis. In 1978 the Foden fleet consisted of two five-axle rigids, four four-axle rigids, seven three-axle rigids and five three-axle tractor units. The company was wound up in the late 1980s.

Declining Sales

Foden sales declined rapidly in the 1970s. The competition with American products became too fierce as American vehicles became extremely popular working tools that were equipped with very powerful engines, large sleeping accommodation and, last but not least, they were very reliable and well suited for Australian conditions. Some truck manufacturers such as the American Kenworth and the Canadian Western Star had set up production facilities in Australia to

Above right: One of the last new Fodens exported to Australia is this 1979 Fleetmaster tipper fitted with a steel S95 day cab, equipped with an air conditioning unit on its roof. This RC29/32 model tipper had a Cummins NTCE290 engine fitted, which was coupled to a Fuller RTO9513 gearbox. It could gross at 64 tonnes when pulling a drawbar trailer. They were assembled by Diesel Motors Ltd of Bentley, Western Australia, which was still Foden's representative at the time. However, the company did not manage to sell new Fodens in Australia after Paccar's acquisition in 1980. *(Author's collection)*

Right: A long wheelbase tractor unit, fitted with the S95 Fleetmaster cab. It was powered by a Cummins NTCE290 engine and could gross at 58 tonnes. It was one of the few Fodens sold in Australia at the end of the 1970s. *(Niels Jansen collection)*

produce custom-built vehicles for the Australian market. At the same time, Volvo and Scania also entered this promising market, resulting in successful sales. Despite several attempts to design purpose-built vehicles for the Australian market, including the Delta-cabbed chassis and the bonneted tractor unit, Foden definitely could not keep up with the competition. In the late 1970s only a handful of rigid eight tippers and some three-axle tractor units fitted with the new steel S95 Motor Panels cab and powered by a Cummins NTCE290 entered the country. They were assembled at Diesel Motors in Bentley (Perth). After Paccar's acquisition of Foden in 1980 hardly any new Fodens were sent to Australia, which meant the end of a major export market. Nevertheless, quite a few Fodens were still running in Australia at the beginning of the 21st century or are restored into new condition, while others are in the progress of an extensive restoration. S18- and S20-cabbed Fodens are particularly popular in Australia now for restoration jobs, although one or two are still earning their keep.

New Zealand

First Imports

Some Foden traction engines and threshing equipment was exported to New Zealand between approximately 1885 and 1925. John Chambers & Son Ltd, which was based in Auckland, imported them.

The Wellington-based Carrick Wedderspoon Co. was Foden's agent in New Zealand before World War II, although not many vehicles were sold to customers in the North or South Island in that period. Luke Brothers of Wellington and Jowett Motors of Auckland also tried to sell Foden vehicles in New Zealand, but they were not very successful either.

Fodenway Motors

As in many Foden export markets, the sales of Fodens really expanded in the 1950s. It was in 1952 that Len Buckby set up a Foden agency in Auckland and Fodenway Motors, as it was appropriately named, soon

imported trucks, buses, crane carriers, dump trucks and two-stroke generators. Len, born in New Zealand, had roamed the world with his wife and children in a 55ft motor sailing vessel from Europe, finally ending up in Africa. He had gained experience with Foden vehicles and Gardner engines in Africa, when he worked as chief engineer and manager for Foden importer Hubert Davies in Bulawayo, Southern Rhodesia. After meeting members of the Foden family in Africa, Len got permission to establish a Foden agency in New Zealand.

Below: Very little is known about this strange-looking tractor unit and even more peculiar semi-trailer. This DG-type tractor unit was exported to New Zealand as a chassis in the late 1940s. It is fitted with a very crude, locally built cab, which features some of the DG cab structure, such as the doors and front mudguards. It was photographed with a trader's plate fitted to the radiator, obscuring its official registration number. *(John Sanderson collection)*

First Post-War Imports

The first vehicles to reach the shores of New Zealand were a batch of lightweight OG4/6 trucks, which were purchased by the Northern Co-operative Carrying Association of Kaitaia. The vehicles had small Gardner 4LK engines fitted, which only produced 57bhp. They were designed to carry 6 tonnes in their drop side bodies, but having such a small engine they struggled to carry these weights. Nevertheless, the company operated seven of these models, which were purchased between 1953 and 1955.

The striking Foden FE4/8 was a promising successor to the slow OG4/6 models. These vehicles, fitted with a stylish aluminium cab, provided payloads of 8 tons. They were powered by Foden's small 2.8-litre, four-cylinder, two-stroke diesel engine, which produced 84bhp. Fodenway Motors sold this model in limited numbers from 1954 to 1956.

S18-cabbed tractor units and rigids were the most successful of the models that entered New Zealand in the 1950s. In contrast with Australian operators, their New Zealand counterparts favoured the two-stroke powered models. As distances and gross weights were generally lower than in Australia, the two-stroke engines had to work less hard in New Zealand, which improved reliability and resulted in longer lives. Many were operated in the logging and timber industry, hauling

Above right: Despite its strange cab, this is definitely a Foden tractor unit, seen here in Fletcher Transport's yard in Patumahoe. The FETU6/20 tractor unit started life in 1954 with a normal S18 cab, but was later fitted with a replacement cab built by Hawke Bros. It was powered by a 126bhp Foden FD6 Mark 2 two-stroke diesel engine. An enlarged external radiator was fitted to provide better cooling. In the last part of its life, fleet number 14 was used for shunting duties. *(Author's collection)*

Right: A second cab replacement was executed by Hawke Bros for another Fletcher-operated FETU6/20 model that carried a consecutive registration number. The fleet number 15 was allocated to DA446. *(Julian Hollinshead)*

sawn timber from the sawmills to the harbours. General hauliers, such as long-time Foden customers Fletchers Transport of Patumahoe, and heavy haulage companies also put quite a few Fodens into service in the 1950s. Fletcher took delivery of its first two Fodens in January 1953. The model FETU6/20 tractor units had Foden Mark I two-stroke engines, producing 126bhp. They were operated sixteen hours a day on two eight-hour shifts.

Foden Buses

The Whenuapai Bus Company of Kumeu put five rear-engined PVRF6 buses into service between 1953 and 1955. They were fitted with locally built bodies by Hawke Bros of Takanini. These bodies accommodated forty-one passengers, with standing for another thirteen. Foden Mark I two-stroke engines powered these remarkable vehicles, which incidentally were the only Foden bus chassis exported to New Zealand. They were operated on Auckland suburban services but they occasionally did trips with tourists to all parts of the country. In 1958 all the buses were sold to the City Bus Service of Napier. As this company and its drivers were not familiar with Foden's two-stroke engines, the vehicles soon developed a reputation for being unreliable. After the company went into liquidation in 1963, the buses were purchased by the Hawkes Bay Motor Company, which completely stripped them and replaced the unreliable Mark I engine with the Mark II. All five buses continued in service and were eventually withdrawn between 1974 and 1979, having been operated for twenty to twenty-five years! And after they were sold off they were bought by members of the public, who converted them into mobile homes. Two of them survived well into the 1990s and one of them had an engine conversion by mounting a Commer TS3 two-stroke diesel engine amidships in the chassis!

Sandliners

To comply with new legislation, which permitted full axle loading without the limitation of the 23-ton gross loading limit, Fodenway Motors, in conjunction with Fodens Ltd, developed three special eight-wheel tippers

in 1961. The customer, Winstones of Auckland, wanted to carry 12 cubic yards on the prime mover and another 10 on a two-axle drawbar trailer, without breaking the contemporary axle load regulations. Foden suggested it could set back both front axles of the standard FE6/24 model tipper and adapt the fibreglass S21 cab for this purpose. The chassis was fitted with eight single wheels, shod with Dunlop 11.00-22 tyres. A Foden six-cylinder

Below: The Whenuapai Bus Company put five PVRF6 rear-engined bus chassis into service between 1953 and 1955. They were fitted with Hawke Bay (Auckland) bodies, which seated forty-one passengers with standing for a further thirteen. One of them, EN6948, is seen here in the ownership of the Hawkes Bay Motor Company, which purchased all five buses in 1963. These had long lives as they were only withdrawn from service between 1974 and 1979. *(Peter Tulloch collection)*

Above: Winstone's three FE6/24 Sandliners were powered by Foden FD6 Mark 3 two-stroke engines, which produced 150bhp. To comply with the latest legislation and provide higher payloads, the front axles of the vehicles were set back. However, the S21 tropical cabs had to be set forward for this axle set-up, which made them look quite different in comparison with standard S21s. The single tyres on the rear bogie of fleet number 204 are clearly visible in this great shot from 1961. *(Fletcher Challenge Archives)*

Left: Winstone's Sandliners were able to pull two-axle drawbar tipper trailers, which improved their payloads to up to 22 cubic yards of sand. Fleet number 202 is loaded here at the Waikato River sand pit by a Michigan 175A wheel loader, while the driver is observing the loading process. The load was destined for Winstone's Vibrapac block plant in Auckland. *(Fletcher Challenge Archives)*

powerful Mark VII two-stroke engine, which produced 225bhp. Fibreglass S24 tilt cabs arrived in New Zealand from 1965 onwards. Pettigrew's Freightways of Napier took delivery of several three-axle trucks coupled to drawbar trailers, which were used for logging and general haulage. Other vehicles went into operation with Fletcher's Transport of Patumahoe, which used Mark VI two-stroke-powered Foden FETU6/20 two-axle tractor units in conjunction with two Dommett single-axle woodchip trailers.

Above: Dales Freightways, based in Auckland, purchased this impressive FCTU6/72 tractor unit in 1965. It was powered by a Cummins NH220 engine, coupled to a Foden twelve-speed gearbox. The 6×4 tractor unit was fitted with the export version of the S20 cab. The massive semi-trailer was nicknamed *Big George* after the founder of the company. The trailer rests on a special jeep dolly, which took quite a lot of weight off the fifth wheel. It also could be extended by placing extra axle rows to move heavy machinery, such as this German-built AEG vessel, which was unloaded at Whangarei Port in 1966. The load was destined for the Marsden Point oil refinery. *(John Sanderson collection)*

4.1-litre FD6 Mark 3 engine, producing 150bhp, matched to a Foden twelve-speed gearbox, powered these remarkable vehicles. All axles of the prime mover were allowed to carry 5 tons, while the drawbar trailer weighed a little over 12 tons fully loaded. Another Sandliner was built and delivered to Waikaia Transport in 1963, but this vehicle was powered by a Foden FD6 Mark 6 engine, which produced 175bhp. Winstone Ltd also purchased nearly forty two-axle and four three-axle dump trucks between 1960 and 1973, all powered by Foden two-stroke engines.

Booming 1960s

Fodenway Motors sold many new Fodens into New Zealand in the booming 1960s. Exports of butter, cheese and lamb to the UK increased every year, which meant that the demand for transport to the major New Zealand ports also increased. At the time, almost 50 per cent of New Zealand exports went to customers in the UK. In the early 1960s most New Zealand-based Fodens had fixed fibreglass S21 cabs fitted. From 1962 onwards quite a few vehicles were fitted with the new and very

Right: Fertiliser and Lime merchants Dibble Bros, based in Te Awamuta on North Island, took delivery of an 8E7/24 model tipper chassis in 1965. The vehicle was fitted with a powerful Foden FD6 Mark 7 two-stroke engine, which developed 225bhp. The engine was coupled to a Foden twelve-speed gearbox, which was more than adequate to keep the truck and drawbar trailer moving in hilly and mountainous terrain. The eight-wheel tipper was fitted with Foden's first tilt cab, the S24, featuring the French rectangular headlamps. *(Author's collection)*

Left: Fletchers of Patumahoe operated quite a few "Chipliners", which pulled double, single axle semi-trailers. The high-sided trailers contained woodchips and sawdust, which was collected from the Carter Kumeu and Carter Holt sawmills and hauled to Fletcher Industries' wallboard plant. Some of the semi-trailers had a four-in-line axle configuration, while others had conventional double tyres fitted to the single axles. This is a 1965 4AE6/30 model, powered by a Foden two-stroke FD6 Mark 6 engine, producing 175bhp. *(Author's collection)*

Left: The Northern Co-operative Carrying Association, based in Kataia, in the northern part of North Island, operated this impressive 6AE7/40 model double drive tractor unit. It pulled a tipping semi-trailer and, to increase payload, an additional small drawbar trailer. It was used for the transport of coal and was powered by the most powerful two-stroke engine that Foden could supply, the FD6 Mark 7 engine producing 225bhp. It dates from 1966 and was fitted with the S24 tilt cab. *(David Bloor collection)*

Right: Owner Reg Jackson and Scotsman Bob Liddell, working for Fodenway Motors of Auckland, pose next to a brand new 1967 Foden 8E7/24 eight-wheel tipper. The vehicle was powered by the famous Foden FD6 Mark 7 two-stroke engine, which developed 225bhp. It is obvious that the vehicle has just been started, hence the visible blue smoke on the right. *(Julian Hollinshead)*

Towards the end of the 1960s the first vehicles fitted with fibreglass S35 tilt cabs and S37 fixed cabs came into the country. One of the operators of such vehicles was Northern Co-operative Carrying Association, which operated three-axle tractor units powered by 200bhp Leyland O680 Power Plus engines. The tractor units pulled two-axle milk tank semi-trailers and additional drawbar trailers.

The demand for higher gross weights resulted in Foden designing special export versions fitted with high-powered engines. As vehicle combinations in New Zealand were allowed to gross at 35 tons at the time, Foden offered three- and four-axle rigids fitted with Cummins NHK220 engines coupled to Foden's twelve-speed gearbox. Some of these vehicles were tested on the demanding steep roads in the High Peak in Derbyshire. An S37-cabbed, three-axle test truck followed the A537 from Macclesfield to Buxton, passing the famous Cat and Fiddle Inn situated at one of the highest peaks. Thanks to the powerful engine, the test vehicle conquered even the steepest 1:6.5 hills without using the lowest ratios in the twelve-speed Foden gearbox. It was equipped with a Jacobs engine brake to achieve safe retardation in mountainous areas.

Fodens Ltd (New Zealand)

The Buckby family owned Fodenway Motors Ltd until 1967. In September of the same year Foden took over the company and renamed it Fodens Ltd (NZ branch). It used the same premises in Great South Road, Auckland. Ted Buckby, son of Len Buckby, was appointed managing director, while Rex Leahy remained sales manager. Foden products were supported by two representatives, one in North Island (Robert Holt & Sons of Napier) and the other one in South Island (Gore Services based in Gore).

Foden sales in New Zealand declined from the mid-1970s onwards, but a number of Cummins-powered S80- and S83-cabbed rigids and tractor units entered the country in the mid and late 1970s. They went into service with loyal Foden operators, including Fletchers Transport, New Zealand Industrial Gases (NZIG) and M. & J. Inglis.

Above: A small number of S41-cabbed Fodens entered New Zealand in the 1970s. It was photographed in 1984, when it was already ten years old. The AC25/60 model tractor unit had a Cummins NHK250 engine fitted that was coupled to a fifteen-speed Fuller Roadranger gearbox. *(Author's collection)*

Right: Despite the declining sales in New Zealand in the 1970s, Fletcher stayed a loyal Foden customer by ordering more Fodens for its transport fleet. A three-axle rigid pulling a four-axle drawbar trailer is on its way delivering fresh produce. Weather conditions were good as there is no sign that the load has been sheeted. The RC25/45 model Foden, fitted with a S83 cab, was built in 1980 and powered by a Cummins NHC250 engine. *(Author's collection)*

Right: New Zealand Industrial Gases (NZIG), which was based in Auckland, operated several S95-cabbed Foden Fleetmasters during the 1980s. This AC29/38 model fitted with steel S95 cab was built in 1979 and powered by a 14-litre Cummins NTCE290 engine. In contrast to the UK versions, the New Zealand S95 cabs had split windscreens fitted. It was one of a fleet of six similar 6×4 tractor units that were operated between Auckland and Lower Hutt on North Island. *(Ben Uncles)*

Opposite: Direct Transport of Rotorua had quite a few Fodens in its fleet. This nicely sheeted 1978 AC29/45 Fleetmaster model was powered by a Cummins NTCE290 engine, coupled to a Fuller RTO909 Road Ranger nine-speed transmission. The tractor unit was fitted with a S95 steel cab produced by Motor Panels. It is seen here in June 1987 parked up at Direct's yard in Rotorua. It was one of at least three similar models operated by this company. *(Rufus Carr)*

Left: S95-cabbed Fleetmaster NZIG 6×4 tractor unit and gas tank semi-trailer. It was exhibited when brand new during a truck show at Auckland in early 1981. Like its sister vehicles, it was an AC33/38 model powered by a Cummins NTK335 engine. NZIG also operated several 4×2 Foden tractor units, fitted with S83 cabs. *(Author's collection)*

FODEN EXPORT VEHICLES

NZIG also purchased a couple of double drive Fleetmaster tractor units in 1979, which were powered by Cummins NTCE290 engines and fitted with S95 steel tilt cabs. In contrast to the UK versions, the New Zealand S95 cabs had split windscreens. The tractor units pulled large capacity gas tank or step frame trailers, depending on whether the gas had to be delivered in bulk or in bottles.

Promising 1980s

After Foden went into receivership, exports to New Zealand nearly came to a halt. Only a handful of Fleetmaster tractor units fitted with the S10 Mark I cab were sold in 1980 to, again, Fletchers Transport and M. & J. Inglis. Between July 1981 and December 1982 there were no export of Fodens to New Zealand. Fortunately, Len Buckby's sons purchased Fodens Ltd (NZ) assets. Ted and John Buckby established a new company, called Specialist Transport Equipment, which eventually became South Pacific Trucks. In 1994 it was renamed Southpac Trucks Ltd. It is not surprising that Southpac Trucks Ltd became the New Zealand Kenworth and DAF importers.

With the introduction of the S104T and S106T tractor units and S106R and S108 rigids in 1983, exports to New Zealand finally increased again. The most popular models, operated in New Zealand, were the S106T 6×4 tractor units and S108R 8×4 rigids, which were adapted for drawbar trailer operations. Most had powerful Cummins or Caterpillar engines to cope with 44-tonne gross combination weights. Due to the relatively low axle weights, which were legally permitted, the truck/trailer combinations needed seven or eight axles to comply with these regulations. That is the reason why New Zealand rigid eight/drawbar combinations look very impressive, which is enhanced by the attractive liveries that are applied to most vehicles. Tractor units can also be seen in New Zealand in A-train configuration (tractor unit, semi-trailer and drawbar trailer) or B-train (tractor unit pulling two semi-trailers).

Right: The driver of this S106T double drive tractor unit poses very willingly in front of his remarkable vehicle. The 1985 model is pulling a conventional two-axle semi-trailer and a smaller two-axle drawbar trailer, both in BP livery. It had a S10 Mark 3 day cab fitted, which had wire-netting windscreen protection. A powerful Cummins NTE350 engine was sufficient to keep this 44-tonne gross combination moving. *(Author's collection)*

Opposite top: Fletcher's Chipliner fleet number 28 is an AC29/40 model fitted with S10 Mark 1 cab and powered by a Cummins NTCE290 engine. JQ2614 was built in 1980 and could gross at 42 tons when pulling four-in-line trailers. *(Author's collection)*

Opposite below: The new S106T tractor units, fitted with the S10 Mark 3 cab, became quite popular in New Zealand during the 1980s. New Zealand Industrial Gases (NZIG) was one of the first customers to put them into service in the country. This 1983 S106T 6×4 tractor unit is pulling a two-axle tank trailer containing highly flammable LPG (liquefied petroleum gas). Fleet number F1343 was powered by a Cummins NTE350 engine. *(Author's collection)*

Left: Waiotahi Transport Ltd, based in the village of Whakatane at the Bay of Plenty in North Island, operated several Fodens. One of them was this S108 model dating from 1985. The vehicle was also operated by James Bull of Hunterville in livestock form. The Cummins NTE350-powered tipper was fitted with an S10 Mark 3 day cab. *(Ben Uncles)*

Right: This magnificent shot of fleet number 3, called the *Kapuni Concord*, was taken in 1986 when the vehicle was new. It was one of four similar 6×4 tractor units that had been delivered to the Lactose Company of New Zealand, based in Kapuni. All tractor units were fitted with the big 16-litre Gardner 6LYT turbo engine, which produced 350bhp. In practice, these engines proved to be quite unreliable and most were replaced by Cummins or Caterpillar engines later. Only a handful were exported to New Zealand. *(Author's collection)*

Left: Some S108 models operated as tractor units in the New Zealand logging industry. This Caterpillar 3406B-350-powered tractor unit dates from 1986. It was equipped with a heavy log-loading crane, which was mounted on the tractor unit. The S108T model was operated by Rex Smith of Taupo (North Island) and was seen at a weighbridge in a forest. *(Author's collection)*

Left: ASC Flowers Transport, based in Wiri, just south of Auckland, operated this wonderful S106R model dating from 1986. It was powered by a Caterpillar 3406B-350 and fitted with the S10 Mark 3 cab. Fleet number 41 pulled a five-axle flatbed drawbar trailer. ASC Flowers ceased trading in July 1993. *(Ben Uncles)*

Left: Livestock operators frequently used rigid eight drawbar combinations. Most outfits had flatbed bodies, which could be loaded quickly with lightweight aluminium livestock crates. Inglewood Motors operated this nice 1987 S108 model, which had a Caterpillar 3406B-400 engine and S10 Mark 3 day cab fitted. Note the phrase painted on the vehicle's front bumper: "If it ain't a CAT it's a dog"! *(Ben Uncles)*

4000 series

Soon after the introduction of the 4000 series models in Great Britain in 1987, they also became available in New Zealand and became very popular. One of the major attractions was the low tare weight and the installation of high-powered American engines, such as the Cummins N14. These engines initially produced 350bhp, but they were uprated to 525bhp in the 1990s. Caterpillar 3406-engines were also on offer, ranging from 350 up to 455bhp. The 4000 series was fitted with S10 Mark 4 (1987–95) and Mark 5 (1995–2001) cabs. The Mark 4 cab was fitted with a new grille panel in 1992 but was not introduced in New Zealand until the

Below: This eye-catching Laing tipper combination worked from Christchurch, South Island, and was put into service in spring 1988. The eight-wheeler was fitted with a Domett–Fruehauf aluminium tipper body and alloy wheels. The three-axle drawbar trailer and tipper body were also manufactured by Domett–Fruehauf. The S108-4350 model featured the new 4000 series S10 Mark 4 cab and was powered by a Caterpillar 3406B-350 engine. *(Author's collection)*

Above: The 4000 series soon became very popular in New Zealand, especially with logging contractors. This nicely painted S106R-4350 model was new in 1988 and carries a decent load. It was operated by Webber Transport of Te Puke, North Island. Fleet number 2 was fitted with a high roof S10 Mark 4 sleeper cab and powered by a Caterpillar 3406B-350 engine. The front axle was shod with wide super single tyres. *(Author's collection)*

Right: PGF Transport Ltd, based in Barneydale, operated many 4000 series Fodens during the 1990s. This spectacular curtain-sided B-train was pulled by a S106T-4450 model, which dates from 1991. It was fitted with the high roof S10 Mark 4 sleeper cab featuring a heavy bull bar. A Caterpillar 3406B-425 engine provided ample power for this type of operation. *(Ben Uncles)*

Left: This drawbar outfit is loaded with some huge grabs, which are fitted to large harbour or industrial cranes. The load sits on a S108-4450 rigid eight and drawbar trailer, operated by Regal Haulage of Hamilton, North Island. The company started in 1988 and now operates 112 trucks and trailers and employs more than 170 people. It is still privately owned. Fleet number 61 was powered by a Caterpillar 3406B-425 engine. *(Ben Uncles)*

FODEN EXPORT VEHICLES

Left: This S108R4-4410 model was put into service by PGF Transport Ltd in 1993, but was later sold to Schreiber Transport, based in New Plymouth, North Island. The Cummins N14-powered truck still carries the personalised registration number PGF9 of its former owners. It carries a nice, roped load consisting of empty wooden cable reels. It features the revised S10 Mark 4 sleeper cab in a raised roof Hi-Line specification. *(Ben Uncles)*

Right: Silver Liner was the name of this S108R4-4465 operated by Godfrey Holdings Ltd of Rotorua (North Island). Fleet number 12 was put into service in 1993 and is seen here at a saw mill waiting for a load of woodchips or sawdust, which would be dropped into the high-sided aluminium bodies. The chip liner had a Cummins NTAA465 engine and a S10 Mark 4 Hi-Line sleeper cab fitted. Godfrey's favoured Foden trucks throughout the 1990s. *(Ben Uncles)*

Left: This is one of five similar high-powered S108R4-4500 trucks purchased in 1994 by Cochrane Transport Ltd. It had depots in Auckland, Cambridge and Mount Maunganui at the time. The nicely sheeted Hi-Line day-cabbed Foden was powered by a Cummins N500E. *(Ben Uncles)*

Opposite: Rapid Transport from Rangiora near Christchurch operated this Caterpillar 3406E-455 powered S108R4-4455 livestock truck pulling a four-axle drawbar trailer. Despite being twelve years old, the combination still really looked nice for its age. It was captured on film by the author while descending Arthur's Pass towards the west coast of South Island on State Highway 73 in November 2008. *(Wobbe Reitsma)*

Right: Only a handful of 3000 series Fodens were exported to New Zealand. The 3000 series was fitted with the narrow version of the S10 cab, which were not popular with big drivers. This is a S106R3-3350 model from 1995, which was operated by Rapid Transport of Rangiora. The truck and drawbar trailer were equipped with livestock crates fitted to their flatbed bodies. A 10-litre Cummins L350E powered this remarkable day-cabbed outfit. *(Ben Uncles)*

FODEN EXPORT VEHICLES

Left: A model S108R4-4425 from 1995 has just entered a large woodchip mill to unload its logs. The Caterpillar 3406B-425-powered vehicle was operated by Cliff Hair Ltd. A large pile of woodchips can be seen in the background. The mill and chip heaps were separated by a tall partition wall. *(John Sanderson collection)*

Right: This 1996 Foden rigid eight had been stretched to the limit and was fitted with an additional lift axle in front of the rear bogie in order to build a heavy Palfinger PK60002 loading crane at the back of the 10×4 driven vehicle. The crane could lift 20ft containers on and off both the truck and drawbar trailer. The S108R4-4425 model was operated by MacKenzie Transport and was photographed in November 2008 on State Highway 1 in Orewa, North Island. *(Wobbe Reitsma)*

Above: Hamley Logging of Putaruro, North Island, operated this well-loaded S108R4-4455 eight-wheeler. The 1997-built truck was fitted with a S10 Mark 5 Hi-Line day cab and powered by a Caterpillar 3406E-455 engine. A huge Komatsu WA800 wheel loader was able to unload both truck and drawbar trailer combination in one single grab. One of the worn out wheel loader tyres obviously acts as a marker for positioning the combination. *(Ben Uncles)*

Left: Foden fire engines are quite rare but this S106R4-4425 model is operated by the New Zealand Refining Company at Marsden Point near Whangarei on North Island. It is powered by a Cummins N14-425 engine coupled to a six-speed Allison automatic gearbox. The body, manufactured by Bronto in Finland, is a Skylift F20WFT aerial extinguisher. *(Ben Uncles)*

Right: Herberts Transport, based in Edendale, South Island, operated this beautiful S108R4.C12-450 model. It features the last version of the S10 Mark 5 Hi-Line day cab, which is fitted with an Alpha-type grille panel. The Caterpillar C12-450 powered eight-wheeler pulled a four-axle drawbar trailer, both fitted with demountable livestock crates to allow it to run as a flatbed or tipper if needed. *(Ian Moxon)*

Above: Woodley's Transport of Geraldine, South Island, operated this striking S108R4.N14-525E livestock combination from 1999. The company specialises in livestock and bulk cartage, but also in fertiliser spreading and agricultural contracting services. There are murals on the sides of the combination depicting farm equipment, trucks and construction equipment. The Foden is powered by a Cummins N525E engine and fitted with a S10 Mk5 sleeper cab featuring the Alpha-type grille panel. *(Ian Moxon)*

following year. Foden dominated the New Zealand six- and eight-wheel rigid market during the greater part of the 1990s. In this decade the S106T4 (6×4 tractor unit) and S108R4 (8×4 rigid truck) were still the most popular models on the New Zealand market. The S106R4 (6×4 rigid truck) was also sold in reasonable numbers. Finally, a very limited number of 3000 series 6×4 tractor units and 6×4 and 8×4 rigid trucks found their way to New

Zealand in 1997 and 1998. They were not popular, probably due to their narrow cabs.

Although the new Alpha series was introduced in 1998, many 4000 series trucks were exported to New Zealand until June 2001, when production of the Mark 5 series 4000 S10 cab finally ceased due to the closure of the Sandbach factory. Production of the Alpha series was transferred to Leyland in Lancashire.

Below: This well-loaded S108R4.N14-525 model features one of the last 4000 series cabs, which was built at Sandbach in 2001. It was photographed in April 2003 at the Rainbow Mountain weighbridge on the road from Murupara to Rotorua, North Island. It was one of a number of Foden vehicles operated by Rotorua Forest Haulage (RFH). The vehicle has a S10 Mark 5 cab and was powered by a 14-litre Cummins N14 engine, producing 525bhp. *(Richard Tew)*

Alpha Series

The first vehicle of this new truck series entered New Zealand in 1999. As 4000 series cabs were still quite popular with New Zealand operators, the new Alpha series fitted with an adapted DAF 85-series cab slowly gained a part of the truck market. Sales went up in 2001 when the 4000 series was no longer available and the MAN-ERF organisation decided to withdraw ERFs from all export markets, including New Zealand. Again, the 6×4 tractor unit (A3.6T model) and the 8×4 rigid (A3.8R model) became the most popular vehicles with New Zealand operators. They could be fitted with Cummins M11.380 or 405 engines or Caterpillar C12-430 engines. Sales of Alpha vehicles in New Zealand increased significantly in 2002, the majority fitted with Caterpillar C12 engines.

The second generation Alpha truck series was introduced in Great Britain in July 2001.

They were fitted with the latest and highly comfortable DAF 85CF-series cab, which became available in day cab, sleeper cab and XL sleeper cab. The interior was improved with a wrap-around dashboard, incorporating an LCD driver information panel, and could be ordered in luxurious wood and leather trims, normally fitted to luxury cars. Paccar's engineers redesigned the exterior of the DAF 85CF cab to create a real Foden look.

Above right: Quality Bakers of Christchurch, which is part of the Goodman Fielder Group, was formed in 1968 by eight medium-sized bakeries. This impressive drawbar combination, fitted with Thermo King-powered refrigerated van bodies, delivered bakery products daily. A Caterpillar C12-430 engine provided ample power for this A3.8R.C12-430 model that dates from 2000. The Alpha day-cabbed vehicle was fitted with shiny alloy wheels. *(Ben Uncles)*

Right: A Foden Alpha Mark 1 heavy haulage tractor unit, pulling a four-axle low-loader loaded with a prefabricated concrete construction. The A3.6TT.C12-430 model was operated by Smith Cranes and Construction company from Christchurch. The tractor unit was built in 2000 and powered by a Caterpillar C12-430 engine. Note the registration number YX4005 that is integrated into the "oversize" sign. *(Author's collection)*

Left: Two-axle Foden tractor units are quite rare in New Zealand as most Fodens have the 6×4 or 8×4 configuration. This one was most likely imported second-hand from the UK. It was operated by Refrigafreighters of Auckland and was, of course, pulling a fridge semi-trailer. The company transported meat, fruit, vegetables and other chilled or frozen products with its fleet of thirty trucks. This is a A3.4T model dating from around 2001, powered by either a Caterpillar C10-380 engine or a Cummins M11.380. *(Ben Uncles)*

Right: Fonterra Dairies operated a very large fleet of eight-wheel milk tankers, pulling four-axle drawbar tank trailers throughout New Zealand. Fonterra was formerly known as New Zealand Milk Products, which was an amalgamation of smaller dairies, such as Anchor's. The Cummins ISM410E-powered vehicle was built in 2001. Fleet number 771 was seen in December 2008 on State Highway 1 in Ashburton on South Island. The Foden Alpha Mark 1 tankers were replaced by Scania and Volvo trucks. *(Wobbe Reitsma)*

Left: West Otago Transport is based in the small village of Heriot on South Island. It specialises in livestock transport, fertiliser spreading and bulk cartage but it also has a daily service for general haulage to Dunedin. One of West Otago's livestock trucks is this very nice A3.8R.C12-430 model, powered by a Caterpillar C12-430 engine. The day-cabbed Alpha Mark 1 dates from 2001. *(Ben Uncles)*

Right: Sutherland Transport Ltd of Waikaka, South Island, operated this nice livestock combination. It is a 2002 model A3.8R.C12-430 powered by a Caterpillar C12-430 engine, which was coupled to an eighteen-speed Roadranger gearbox. Fleet number 3 has four-deck livestock crates fitted to its flatbed body and drawbar trailer. *(Author's collection)*

Right: Another A3.8R.C12-430 model eight-wheeler is seen here parked up at Watchorn's yard at Whakatane near the Bay of Plenty on North Island. The Alpha model, which was built in 2000, shows a neatly chained down load of timber. The sheets, which can be seen in an open locker just below the truck's flatbed deck, were obviously not necessary on that particular sunny day. *(Richard Tew)*

Opposite: A beautiful livestock combination that operated from Te Anau at the borders of Lake Te Anau in central Fiordland, South Island, from where tourists can explore the spectacular Milford Sound. Te Anau Bulk Haulage has operated quite a few Fodens. This, number 22, is one of several Alpha Mark 1s in the fleet, powered by a Caterpillar C12-430 engine. *(Ben Uncles)*

Left: Four-axle tractor units became popular in New Zealand in the first decade of the 21st century. To gross at 44 tonnes they needed eight axles, hence the four-axle semi-trailer. This Caterpillar C12-450 powered unit, dating from 2002, probably started life as a rigid and was converted later into a tractor unit. It was operated by Container Transport & Storage (CTS), which operated several Alpha Mark 1 and 2 Fodens. *(Author's collection)*

Right: Q Transport, based in Waitara, specialises in container services and machinery transport. It also has a depot in Tamaki, Auckland. This nice five-axle 10×4 rigid dates from approximately 2002 and was powered by a Cummins ISM11.440E engine. The fifth axle has been added to carry the weight of the big HIAB loading crane. The load exists of a heavy generator provided by Devon Hire of New Plymouth, which is a major supplier of generators and pumping equipment to the gas and oil industries. *(Ben Uncles)*

Opposite: Plains Transport of Christchurch operated this 2004 double drive tractor unit powered by a Cummins ISM420E engine. Fleet number 408 was contracted to BP New Zealand and encountered by the author at a petrol station in the city centre of Blenheim, South Island, on 23 November 2008. The tare weight of the A3.6T.ISM420E model tractor unit was only 8,300kg. *(Wobbe Reitsma)*

Left: Despite being introduced in the UK in 2001, the Second Generation Alphas did not enter New Zealand before August 2003. Clark & Rogers of New Plymouth, North Island, operated this immaculate model A3.8R.C12-450. It was built in 2003 and powered by a Caterpillar C12-450 engine. This new day-cabbed Alpha transported animal feed stuffs on contract for NRM, which is part of the worldwide Heinz consortium. *(Ben Uncles)*

Left: Eight-wheelers, pulling big drawbar trailers, are immensely popular in New Zealand. These impressive outfits can gross at 44 tonnes. Fleet number 118 is a Caterpillar C12-450-powered A3.8R. C12-450 model from 2004, operated by Tranzfreight of Taupo, based in the central part of North Island. *(Ben Uncles)*

Right: A nice Alpha Mark 2 tractor unit, pulling two milk tank semi-trailers at speed. The tractor unit had a personalised registration number fitted, which immediately reveals the engine and power rating. The A3.6T.C12-450 double drive tractor unit, operated by Reads Transport of Te Puke, North Island, is, of course, powered by a Caterpillar C12-450 engine. It has also been operated in the Dairy Fresh livery as fleet number 108. *(Author's collection)*

Left: A brand new Alpha model A3.8R.C12-450 in February 2005. It was operated by McNab Transport Ltd, based in Gore, and used on livestock transport around the lower part of South Island. Like most New Zealand Alphas, it had a Caterpillar C12-450 engine. McNab Transport Ltd is owned and operated by Roy Agnew but is also involved in lime bulk spreading and household water supplies. *(Ian Moxon)*

Right: The very first four-axle tractor unit to enter New Zealand was purchased by Strait Line Haul Ltd, based in Wellington, North Island, at the beginning of 2005. It pulled a 46ft Maxicube semi-trailer equipped with a King refrigerator. The tractor unit was fitted with a standard sleeper cab and was powered by a Caterpillar C12-450 engine. It was seen in February 2005 in Westfield (Auckland). Strait Line Haul operated a night trunk service between Auckland and Wellington. *(Ian Moxon)*

Above: After the successful introduction of the Alpha Mark 1 into the Fonterra milk collection fleet, more orders for the Mark 2 version followed soon. Fleet number 310 was powered by a Cummins ISM420E engine and was encountered at a petrol station just outside Rotorua on State Highway 5. *(Wobbe Reitsma)*

FODEN EXPORT VEHICLES

Above: An impressive Watchorn Alpha Mark 2 fully loaded with logs. The company has operated several Alpha Mark 1 and 2 trucks and is based in Whakatane in the Bay of Plenty, North Island. Fleet number 4 was a model A3.8R.C12-450 dating from 2005. It was fitted with a day cab and powered by a Caterpillar C12-450 engine. *(Ian Moxon)*

Left: Whitehead Transport took delivery of the first XL-cabbed Alpha tractor unit. The 3+2 B-train runs on contract for Mainfreight. It was photographed during the Mystery Creek truck show in March 2005. A Caterpillar C12-450 engine powered this A3.6T.C12-450XL model. Mainfreight mainly uses owner-drivers and small fleets for its freight services. That is why the tractor units XL-cab carry the message: "Special people – special company". *(Ian Moxon)*

be introduced. However, the 44-tonne legislation was still in existence in 2016.

Papua New Guinea

One of the first Fodens to be operated in the former Australian part of New Guinea entered service in the early 1950s. The S18-cabbed boxvan 4×2 rigid vehicle was operated by the Bulolo Gold Dredging Co. Ltd (BGD), which operated a fleet of Fodens well into the 1960s. The company operated eight mining dredges to look for alluvial gold in the Bulolo Valley. The Fodens hauled equipment, fuel and food from Lae to the Bulolo Valley. BGD also became involved with forestry when it took a 50 per cent share in the New Guinea Timber Ltd; the Australian government owned the other 50 per cent of the shares. Several FG-type four-wheelers and eight six-wheel Fodens fitted with Gardner 6LW engines were purchased in the early 1950s to transport the plywood from the mill to the coast, from where it was shipped.

In 1969 Lae Markham Transport (LMT) put an impressive drawbar outfit into service. LMT operated a three-axle flatbed rigid Foden 6C6/22 fitted with a S41 sleeper cab and Cummins NHK250 diesel engine. The routes, which had to be conquered, were corrugated and full of potholes, and some gradients were quite severe. The vehicle was operated in the Western Highlands of New Guinea between Lae, Goroka and Mount Hagen. The truck combination had to negotiate a gradient between Goroka and Mount Hagen that rose more than 3,000ft in 9 miles. The two-axle drawbar trailer sometimes had to be uncoupled in the mountainous areas due to the badly maintained roads. An additional

It included a new grille panel, incorporating the well-known Foden kite. The flat doors were another typical Foden feature. Many New Zealand trucks still have day cabs fitted, because drivers who are in their vehicles are classed as being on duty. That is the reason why New Zealand trucks are not double-manned either. Most drivers return to base at the end of their working day or hand over their truck to another driver and stay the night in a motel or company-owned house. Another important reason to fit day cabs is the fact that drawbar combinations can handle two more pallets, which, of course, increases productivity.

Production of the new double drive tractors and rigids started in the first quarter of 2002. However, it took until August 2003 before the first vehicles were

exported to New Zealand. The Alpha series was specifically tailored to NZ operators' needs. Owing to the restricted dimensions of the Alpha cab it was not possible to fit Cummins ISX or Caterpillar C-15 engines, which produced high engine outputs in the 500 to 600bhp bracket. The new Alphas became available in 6×4 tractor unit, 6×4 and 8×4 rigid truck chassis, which were powered by either Cummins ISM385E, ISM420E or ISM345/420ESP engines or Caterpillar C12-400 and 450 engines. The New Zealand haulage industry had pleaded for a gross combination weight rise to 50 tonnes for quite some years. During the last two years of Alpha production, several four-axle tractor units emerged in New Zealand. They were obviously prepared for a 50-tonne g.c.w., as soon as this new legislation would

Left: One of the FG6/12 flatbed trucks operated by the Bulolo Gold Dredging Co. in Australian New Guinea. The vehicle dates from 1953 and is about to disembark from a landing craft. It moved food, fuel, equipment and also plywood between Lae and Bulolo, a distance of 90 miles, following the course of Bulolo River until it met Snake River. *(David Bloor collection)*

Right: Vacuum Oil Company of Lae operated this mid-1950s model FG6/12 tanker in Mobilgas livery. Fleet number 2664 delivered oil products from its base in Lae to the Bulolo Valley, climbing mountains up to 2,100ft, fully using its Gardner 6LW, which only produced 112bhp. *(John Sanderson collection)*

spare wheel and tyre was carried on the heavy front bull guard. A round trip from Lae to Mount Hagen involved 660 miles and was carried out three times a week.

New Caledonia

In 1990 Foden appointed Caltrac SA, based in Noumea, as a main dealer. The New Caledonia Islands, which are situated north of New Zealand and east of Australia, produce more than 10 per cent of the world's nickel. Also in 1990, Caltrac sold a number of heavy duty 4000 series six and eight-wheelers fitted with Caterpillar 300 and 350bhp engines, which were coupled to Allison automatic transmissions. All vehicles were equipped with Edbro dump bodies and tipping gear; the tippers operated at gross weights up to 42 tonnes.

Nauru

The island of Nauru is a tiny (21 sq km), independent republic in the middle of the Pacific Ocean. It is situated east of the Melanesian archipelago and just 30 miles south of the equator. The island is a coral reef, which is rich in phosphate and that is why the Nauru Phosphate Company ordered eight Foden FC 27A dump trucks in the early 1970s. The phosphate was mined from opencast sites. The Fodens were kept busy for many years to move the phosphate to the processing plant to be converted into valuable fertiliser. Cummins NT310 engines coupled to Allison automatic transmissions powered these giant, 14 cubic yard, dump trucks, which grossed at 40 tons. They had a hard life in Nauru, being operated twenty-four hours a day in three shifts over dirt tracks. The blown up dirt had to be kept down by frequently spraying salt water. The Fodens did a fine job, resulting in a repeat order for two more dump trucks. The Fodens even featured on a stamp in 1975, commemorating the Nauru Phosphate Corporation's fifth anniversary.

Above: Four of the eight FC27A dump trucks delivered to the Nauru Phosphate Company in the early 1970s. They were powered by Cummins NT310 engines and had Allison automatic transmissions. *(Author's collection)*

CHAPTER SIX

The One and Only

For nearly twenty years I thought that the last Foden sold in Holland was that impressive S90 8×4 model RR22/30 concrete mixer that was sold to the Sagro company in Berkel–Enschot in 1976. After that time there was no importer to represent the famous Sandbach truck manufacturer in Holland.

In 1995 I heard from two different friends that they had seen a new Foden with a Dutch registration number in the central part of Holland. Unfortunately neither managed to write down the number and as the tractor had no sign writing it took another eight months before another friend saw the Foden again. This time he contacted the driver on his CB radio and luckily he was willing to give him his telephone number.

Shortly after my summer holidays, I phoned him up and had a nice chat with him. He confirmed he operated a Foden 4000 series tractor unit, which was pulling a logging semi-trailer. After I had asked permission to photograph the combination, he invited me to come over to the village of Ede on a Saturday morning. I had to meet him at the local Mercedes–Benz truck dealer, where the Foden was serviced regularly.

I met Rolf Kerkhof at this dealer at ten in the morning and the first thing I did was drink coffee with him and the fitters, who were trying to convince him that his next tractor had to be a new Mercedes–Benz Actros. But Rolf could not be convinced that easily.

He told me that he and his partner, Peter, who were both shareholders of the limited company Rondhout Transport Ede BV (Round Timber Transport Ede Ltd), had chosen the Foden very carefully. Rolf, who was a qualified forestry engineer, started the business with Peter at the end of 1994 after an eight-year career as a transport manager at a large company in the area.

Rolf had always favoured Cummins engines and Rockwell axles, and he had also been an enthusiast reader of *Truck Magazine* for a long time. So after rereading some recent Foden road tests he and his partner decided to go for one. The problem was that there was no Foden importer in Holland and that is why he contacted the Foden factory in Sandbach directly. After a couple of visits to Sandbach, where Rolf had long talks with Foden engineers, he was able to tell them what tractor he wanted and for what purposes he needed it. The tractor had to have double drive, a short wheelbase, a low weight, air suspension on the double drive bogie and a fifth-wheel coupling height of 1.2m because the partners also wanted to pull normal semi-trailers. They were not just going into logging and wanted to double shift the Foden when they were asked to pull semi-trailers for Scansped and Malenstein Transport.

They ordered a S106T4-4410 Foden tractor unit, which had a 14-litre Cummins N410 engine with Jacobs engine brake, an Eaton Twin Splitter TSO 15612 gearbox, a Spicer propshaft and a Rockwell double drive bogie with Airtrac air suspension. The chassis was fitted with a 4000 series S10 Mark 4 Hi-Line sleeper cab with double bunks. The 7,900kg GKN front axle in combination with the 23,000kg Rockwell bogie had

Left: The Loglift 200 crane makes easy work of loading the logs, which have been waiting for transportation in a Dutch forest in the central part of Holland. Rolf Kerkhof starts to load the very sophisticated Faymonville semi-trailer with pine. This trailer was manufactured in Belgium and could be extended to 19m. Both second and third axles were hydraulically steered. *(Wobbe Reitsma)*

litres of hydraulic oil in about one minute. The header tank contained 180 litres of hydraulic oil, which means that nearly all the oil was circulated every two minutes; that is why an oil cooler was fitted in front of the header tank.

Before we went off Rolf told me that he more or less designed his own unit and that is another reason why they chose a Foden. According to him, Foden was one of the few manufacturers that was able to custom build the tractor unit and listen to all the ideas and wishes of the operator. The Foden had done more than 220,000km in fewer than twenty months. It was not entirely trouble free, but Rolf was still happy with the performance of the Foden. The only drawback was the downtime when the tractor needed to be repaired in Belgium. Rolf had just changed the Michelin XYZ tyres of the double drive bogie; they lasted 215,000 kilometres and that is very good when you bear in mind that the Foden did a lot of work in the forests.

It was time to load timber in the extensive woodlands in the northern part of the Veluwe area, which is roughly situated between the cities of Amersfoort, Apeldoorn and Zwolle. Rolf had to collect a load of pine which was 10–12m long. It was important to the timber merchant to collect the load on this Saturday because the weather forecast said it was going to rain in the next few days and that could make the pine worthless if it

a lot of technical reserve, although legally the Foden tractor was allowed to do "only" 25,000kg. With an empty weight of only 7,900kg the tractor could take 17,100kg on its fifth wheel. The gross combination weight in Holland for such a tractor–semi-trailer combination was not allowed to exceed the 50,000kg limit.

The Foden was built in December 1994 and delivered to Rolf and his partner by the Belgium Foden importer Eurocamions Ltd. They also ordered a Belgian three-axle semi-trailer, which was built at the Faymonville factory of Bullingen. The company is situated near the German border in the eastern part of the Ardennes hills. The Faymonville KL3 trailer is 13.6m long and can be extended up to 19m to transport trees up to 22m. The whole combination measured a staggering 27.5m. Of

course, such long trailers need to have steering axles; this one was hydraulically steered on the second and third axle. Both axles could also be steered manually from the cab. As the trailer had a chassis it was also capable of transporting short logs. The reinforced aluminium poles could be moved hydraulically from the front of the trailer to the back. The 8m reach of the Finnish Loglift F200SL 20-tonne/metre loading crane was more than adequate to load all kinds of round timber. The timber grab could be rotated 360 degrees. The crane was mounted at the front of the semi-trailer and had two large hydraulic outriggers to stabilise it.

An extensive hydraulic system had been built on to the tractor unit to operate the loading crane, the stabilisers and the steering axles of the semi-trailer. This system was fed by two PTO pumps, which each circulated 80

grew mouldy. The 410bhp Cummins did not have to work very hard with the unladen semi-trailer behind and soon we reached the forest where we had to load the pine.

Rolf told me that we had about a 60 per cent chance of getting stuck on the wet forest tracks and as there was no other forest plant such as farm tractors or shovels available during the weekend, he had to be careful. Before entering the narrow forest track, Rolf made a reconnaissance on foot to spot the weak parts. The pine had been dropped by the cutters at six different places alongside the track. His conclusion was that it was not possible to take the whole load in one go. He opted for a half load, which he could tip at the end of the track near the public road. Then he would go into the forest again, collect another half load and finally reload the first half.

The hydraulically steered trailer axles proved to be a great help when we tried to get into this very narrow track. Rolf had to operate it manually and despite the 10ft width between the trees, he got the semi-trailer into the track in one go. Rolf loaded the first half load of pine very easily. He has gained great experience in operating the Loglift loading crane, many times there was very little room to swing the long trunks and get them on to the trailer properly. Moving from one spot to another was a bit tricky sometimes but luckily the double drive tractor did not get stuck. Of course, Rolf used the differential locks at some soft spots. The only drawback of the Airtrac suspension is, according to Rolf, that this system does not shift weight to the other axle when it gets into a pothole.

The Foden was worked very hard and the cab certainly showed a lot of scratches caused by overhanging branches. However, apart from some small dents in the aluminium doors the dark green tractor still looked good; you can't see all those scratches on the photographs anyway.

After five hours the trailer was finally fully loaded with 38 cu m of pine and it was time to return to base. As there are no weighbridges in the forests, Rolf estimated that the pine weighed about 35 tonnes and the tractor–trailer combination a little over 21 tonnes. That meant that the whole outfit grossed at about 56 tonnes, a little over the legal limit. But that seemed not to be a problem as we had only 25 miles to go.

The Cummins was humming quite satisfactory, but working very hard to keep the 56 tonnes moving. The Jake brake also gave very impressive results when we had to slow down, especially on the narrow roads and in the small villages. Anyway, it was a great experience, as I had never seen a forestry truck in working conditions. And I certainly learned a thing or two from Rolf about forestry and timber trucks. One thing is very clear to me, Rolf certainly is a dedicated Foden man, or should I say Cummins/Eaton/Rockwell man?